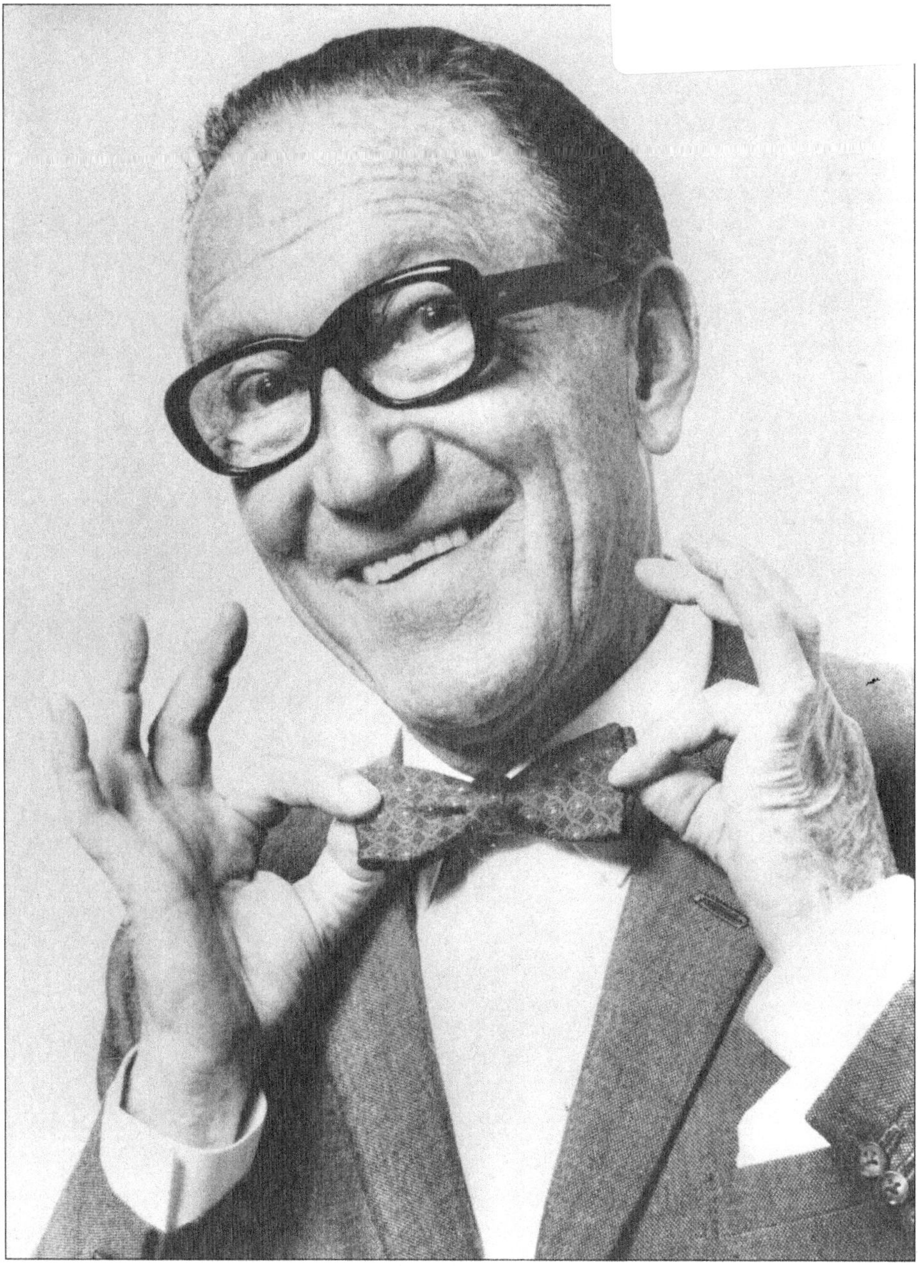

I Thank You:
THE ARTHUR ASKEY STORY

ANTHONY SLIDE

I Thank You: The Arthur Askey Story
© 2020 Anthony Slide. All Rights Reserved.

No part of this book may be reproduced in any form or by any means, electronic, mechanical, digital, photocopying or recording, except for the inclusion in a review, without permission in writing from the publisher.

BearManor Media
1317 Edgewater Drive #110
Orlando, Florida 32804
www.bearmanormedia.com

Hardcover: ISBN 978-1-62933-561-2
Paperback: ISBN 978-1-62933-560-5

Printed in the United States of America.
Book design by Brian Pearce | Red Jacket Press.

Table of Contents

Acknowledgments 7

Introduction 9

CHAPTER ONE: The Early Years 25

CHAPTER TWO: The Beginnings of a Show Business Career 33

CHAPTER THREE: *Band Waggon* 47

CHAPTER FOUR: On Screen 65

CHAPTER FIVE: On Stage 95

CHAPTER SIX: On Television 119

CHAPTER SEVEN: Ol' Man Askey 133

CHAPTER EIGHT: Legacy 141

Bibliography 149

Filmography 153

Index 157

About the Author 161

Acknowledgments

This is a small book about a small man. Appropriately, the acknowledgments page is equally small, with specific thanks to Geoff Brown, Glenn Mitchell, Julian Paltenghi and Michael Pointon.

My partner, Robert Gitt, very kindly scanned for me the photographs that appear in the book. Those photographs come primarily from my own collection, with additional ones provided by the Askey family.

This book would not have happened had it not been for Ben Ohmart and BearManor Media encouraging me to take on the project. I must also thank my production editor, Brian Pearce, who is a reliable and effective expert in his field.

I am most grateful to Arthur's three grandchildren, Jane, Andrew and William. Jane Stewart took considerable time to read the manuscript and provide me with intelligent and helpful comments. Above all, I must thank grandson, William Ewart, who gave me access to the family memorabilia that he safeguards. I am very much aware of the major hassle it was for him to host me while in the process of moving his family from one home to another. Thanks Will!

Arthur Askey's Annual

FEATURING
BIG-HEARTED ARTHUR,
'STINKER' MURDOCH,
NAUSEA & Mrs. **BAGWASH**,
ERNIE BAGWASH,
LEWIS the **GOAT**,
AND OTHER OLD FRIENDS

Introduction

It might be argued that Britain has something of a tradition of diminutive or small men as comedians, "mini-comedians," as they were once described. There are those who always appeared as young boys who never grew up, such as Wee Georgie Wood [1] and Jimmy Clitheroe,[2] on stage, screen and in the latter's case, radio. There is Ronnie Corbett [3] who teamed up with the regular-sized if somewhat overweight Ronnie Barker as "The Two Ronnies" on television and the variety stage. Similarly, on the distaff side, is Gracie West,[4] who teamed up with the lanky Ethel Revnell, billed as "The Long and the Short of It" in in the 1930s and 1940s.

The notion of pint-sized comedians may, perhaps, have originated with Little Tich (Harry Relph),[5] a darling of the music hall, at the height of his fame from the 1880s through the early 1900s, who also enjoyed fame and success in the United States. While some might claim that the greatest of this type of comedian is Ronnie Corbett, certainly a good argument might be made that the genre is best represented by Arthur Askey, a concert party comedian who made an easy transition to radio, films and television.

Wee Georgie Wood, Jimmy Clitheroe and Gracie West all relied on characterizations as children. And it must be noted that there is something strangely uncomfortable watching the thirty-six year-old Wee Georgie Wood leading a gang of children (real children) into mischief in the 1930 film, *The Black Hand Gang*. That one of the young boys actually appears in the nude does not exactly ease one's discomfort. Jimmy Clitheroe made only a handful of films, primarily in the 1940s and 1950s, and is best known for the BBC radio series, *The Clitheroe Kid*, heard from 1958-1972. It must be wondered why it was necessary to have a midget play a child on radio, the audience for which would not have been aware of the actor's height.[6] But then again, one of the most popular entertainers on BBC Radio was Peter Brough, a ventriloquist famed for his dummy,

Archie Andrews, and the art of ventriloquism can hardly be practiced on the radio. Indeed, one wonders if perhaps a good partnership for the BBC might have been Peter Brough with Jimmy Clitheroe as the live equivalent of the dummy.

Arthur Askey was five feet, two inches in height, a foot taller than Jimmy Clitheroe and five inches taller than Wee Georgie Wood. He was also a far superior comedian. He didn't play kids, although he did play female roles, primarily as a pantomime dame on stage and in the 1940 film, *Charley's (Big-Hearted) Aunt*. Arthur does seem rather to enjoy putting on a dress, albeit never a glamorous one and absolutely never with an emphasis on feminity.

As that film's title proclaims, what Arthur Askey lacked in height, he made up for in big-heartedness. Here was a diminutive comedian, almost pixie-like, who proved that good things can come in small packages. There was a natural exuberance to Askey's performances in all media. He always gave the impression of being a fun guy to be around, with no chip on his shoulder and no bitterness as to his height as might be suggested and often confirmed by Wee Georgie Wood and Jimmy Clitheroe. Unfortunately, not all good things come in small packages. One British entertainer once explained Wee Georgie Wood's often negative personality to me by observing that small people had a problem in that their brains were too close to their bottoms. Askey would not agree with this assessment, claiming that being short kept him going as the blood didn't have as far to go around his body. He also pointed out,

"I think a short comic is at an advantage because he has the audience's sympathy right away. I think on the whole being short has been a great asset for me in my career."[7]

"Hello, playmates," said Askey. "It's all right — you're not being diddled. This is all there is!" As John Fisher has written in his definitive history of British comedy, *Funny Way to Be a Hero*:

"His sheer physicality as he rolled his shoulders up and down, projected his elbows like jug handles, protruded his posterior and did his funny little shuffle like a speeded-up figure on a Swiss clock only emphasized the lack of inches."[8]

"Did you ever see such a funny little bloke as me?" Askey would ask his audience, even including the question in a 1941 song of his, "The Pixie." And the answer was a resounding "No." There was absolutely zero competition with the likes of any other "little blokes" from his era in entertainment.

There were many who were familiar with Askey only through radio and unaware of his height. The comedian recalled attending a screening of his film version of *The Ghost Train*:

"I had become a big star on radio but obviously the public could not see me or realise I was very short. I jumped at the chance to become a movie star and when the film was released I crept into a cinema and sat behind two ladies, hoping to hear the compliments flow.

"When the film was over, one of them turned to the other and said, 'he was quite funny but I never realised he was deformed,' and that certainly burst my ego bubble."[9]

No-one could suggest that Askey was a particularly attractive-looking comedian. Apart from his height — of itself not a detraction — he wore thick, black, horn-rimmed glasses, he had red hair slicked back in military style, his features were undeveloped, and he looked pale with his face covered in freckles and liver spots.

Askey seldom, if ever, wore outlandish or oddly-fashioned clothing (except, of course, when in character in pantomime). In the 1930s and 1940s, he did sport a strange-looking hat, which might have suited Robin Hood or a member of his merry band, and the origins of which are a mystery.

Apropos the glasses, Arthur Askey was one of a small group of British performers who was never seen without them. Harry Worth and Sandy Powell were two other bespectacled comedians, who, like Askey, wore them because they needed them — not because they were props. To a certain extent, Eric Morecambe of Morecambe and Wise would fiddle with his glasses for effect. Commentator Eric Midwinter has pointed out that the only comedian recognized as much for his glasses as anything else was Will Hay: "His films and their recent revivals on television mean that another generation now recognizes the wispy hair, the slightly slack mouth and the snub nose of Will Hay. But the recognition is primarily due to the pince-nez."[10]

In performance, Arthur Askey exuded what appeared to be a natural exuberance and self-confidence. "Acting to me is like breathing in and out — it's no effort at all," he once commented.[11] Askey was larger than life on stage because he had to be. He was irrepressible and lovable, with the audience perhaps feeling a warm-hearted glow towards him because of his size. He could never be threatening and never have an audience in fear of him. Never a suggestion that he might single out a member of the audience for ridicule. His manner was welcoming and the public responded accordingly. There was no pretense here, no suggestion that he was superior to any of his peers.

As one commentator wrote after Askey's death,

"Unlike many of those who followed, there was no malice in those twinkling eyes behind the thick-rimmed glasses. Although perhaps difficult to believe in this day and age, everybody liked him and he appealed to all age groups — right across the board."[12]

There was nothing really special about Arthur Askey's act. He would come on stage and have a conversation with the audience. The conversation just happened to be comprised of a series of jokes. There was nothing particularly original about the humor. "Excuse me laughing, but I know what is coming," he would tell his audience. He could always be relied upon to take the mickey out of the joke. As Askey remarked in the 1970s, "I'm using the same material that I used fifteen years ago. I put the gags in a different order."[13] The material might be ancient, but as one commentator pointed out in the 1960s, it was "totally irresistible and indefatigably contemporary."[14] The gags might be old, but as early as April 1932, *The Monthly Pictorial* described Askey as "The Modern Comedian." To most observers, he seemed brilliant at "off the cuff" humor as Peter Black in *TV Mirror* (March 26, 1955) pointed out. Like Arthur himself, every joke was a little gem. Arthur Askey was there to be funny, but as he was anxious to point out,

"Being funny is not always merely making fun. The man who makes fun must have a butt. He makes fun at someone else's expense. To a few people it may be humour, but I cannot look at it just in that way. There is some little quirk in my nature which always reminds me that if I make one person or a group of persons a butt for a joke, that person or the members of this group suffer. So I try to keep all my humour free from this sort of influence because, to tell the honest truth, I don't like to see people suffering or to think of them suffering."[15]

While there might be a natural spontaneity to his performances, Askey did write down notes for his act, and sometimes the complete act, in exercise books. Later, when he was a member, he would utilize Garrick Club notepaper. He wrote a substantial number of sketches and even complete, short pantomimes, but they do not appear to have been produced. Extant radio and television scripts contain minor changes in his hand, but from a modern perspective, they add little if anything to the specific programs.

Askey commented that he wrote much of his own material, stealing it or twisting it as necessary:

"I've never been in the happy position of Tony Hancock with [writers] Galton and Simpson, or Jimmy Edwards with Muir and Norden. Tony was a great character comedian, but try to push him on without a script if the safety curtain was stuck — which has happened with me — and he couldn't fill in. Jimmy could do it…especially if he had a gin or two.

"I've also got in my ancestry a good singing voice and a musical ability. I can play the piano. And I dance a bit.…I can do nearly everything. Except Shakespeare, although I have been asked several times to play Bottom."[16]

Askey also maintained that there was nothing crude or vulgar in his act, commenting that the joke "may not be funny, but it's clean." In fact, this is somewhat untrue. It all depends on one's interpretation of "clean." Is the following dialogue with Richard Murdoch from World War Two questionable, crude or simply homophobic:

"Who was that lady I saw you with last night?"

"That was no lady. That was my nephew. He walks that way."

A sampling of Askey's jokes from 1972 indicate that he was keeping up with modern and suggestive humor:

"This wealthy dame had her face lifted so many times — she had to start shaving."

"Young widow walking down the street in a bright yellow dress. 'I thought you'd be in mourning as your husband has only just passed away.' She lifted her skirt and showed she had a pair of black panties on. 'I wear my mourning where I miss him most.'"

"Two policemen walking home — one says — when I get home, I'm going to tear the wife's knickers off — they're killing me!"

Perhaps a critic in the *Aberdeen Press and Journal* (August 22, 1944) had it right when he wrote that Askey was "clever without seeming so, and sly in the spice."

Askey belonged to an era of comedy in which the comedy style was more innuendo and naughty rather than blatant.

Despite his denial of crudeness or vulgarity in his act, Askey did end his screen career with *Rosie Dixon — Night Nurse*, a sex exploitation film in which his entire time is spent pinching women's bottoms. Granddaughter Jane notes that Arthur never saw the entire script and did not know the subject matter, but only the pages covering his cameo part. "I think he was reasonably happy to film it, but was pretty horrified when he saw the whole movie."[17]

Certainly, the film is not as crude as the "Carry On" productions, but Askey's performance suggests that he might well have found a niche there as a character comedian. (Of course, the reality is that Askey was too big a comedy star to be a member of the "Carry On" brigade, and it is extremely doubtful that the producer would have even considered the fee the comedian would expect.)

A critic with the *Reading Mercury* in 1939 perceptively pondered the question of Askey's popularity with audiences while watching his twenty-minute act:

"What makes a great comedian? What is it that has brought fame to Charles Chaplin, George Robey, Max Miller and now Arthur Askey. Each has found distinction in his own particular way, but it is not easy to account for Arthur Askey's tremendous popularity. Judged on his remarkably successful visit to the Odeon Theatre, Reading, on Sunday, he has not climbed the ladder on the rungs of original humour. So many of his jokes were traditional that a lesser man would have cracked them in silence. Thunderous applause and gales of laughter were Arthur Askey's reward, and it seems that to be a first-rate entertainer it does not matter so much what is said as the way it is put over.

"I know I'm a concert party comedian, but I'm as good as any of them," asserted Askey. Fellow comedian Ted Ray agreed, but added,

"That is true. I'm a typical music hall comedian, he is more a gentle comedian who plays to gentle audiences at the seaside while I was fighting for my life on the hall in [the North of Enland, working class city of] Sunderland.

"Arthur in Bournemouth or Shanklin was playing to people on holiday. But who goes to Sunderland on holiday?....They were on their holidays. They had been on the sands. Now they were going to be entertained by this funny little man — I always call him a large dwarf. Arthur would make it with the audience on Monday. It took me until Wednesday."[18]

"That is another way of saying that one must have personality, and there is no doubt that 'Big-Hearted Arthur' possesses more than an ordinary share of that gift. He had the record audience 'in his lap' on Sunday from the moment he ran on the stage."[19]

The comedian was never still on stage, always prancing around, often indulging in eccentric dance routines, which would sometimes give the impression of being choreographed and sometimes not. As one contemporary critic noted he was like the busy bee of which he sang. Every movement had a comedic aspect to it — it might be unrehearsed, but Askey knew how to move, when to move, and how to use that movement to appeal to his audience. As Ken Dodd has pointed out, watching Arthur Askey was like watching a fireworks display go off. "so much energy, so much life."[20]

When Askey came to national fame with *Band Waggon*, his energy level did not diminish either on and off stage. It was reported that a fifteen to eighteen hour day was nothing to Arthur.[21]

At least through the 1930s, the movement was not limited to his lower half, as his hands seem to be in constant motion as he tells a joke. Always, it seemed that Askey was enjoying himself as much as his audience. As he proudly boasted, he never suffered from stage fright. When Askey went off to make his first pantomime appearance, he wrote in his autobiography that "I felt completely confident."[22]

Unlike, say Norman Wisdom or Chaplin, there was never any sense of pathos in Askey's routine. There were certainly reviewers who felt Askey's act might be improved with the addition of some pathos to calm down the non-stop attack of jokes. He recalled that the great theatre critic James Agate had once told him he might be a great comedian if he was to add pathos to his make-up. Askey responded,

"But I don't want pathos. It hurts me. I don't want pathos at all. I like to be happy. I've always tried to give the impression that I'm being happy and want to make other people happy. I don't want to do [singing] 'Don't laugh at me...' or anything like that."[23]

If audiences wanted pathos from a little man in the 1930s there was always the great — the very great — German tenor, Josef Schmidt, whose mere existence in Nazi Germany is of itself pure pathos. In Schmidt's best-known film, *My Song Goes round the World* (1934), the four foot, eleven inches tall singer is told by his leading lady words to the effect that he is a little man and nobody can love a little man. Arthur Askey certainly never had that problem in that he was genuinely loved as an entertainer at the height (no pun intended) of his career.

No song could be performed with Askey standing quietly at center stage. In the 1920s (or at least so he claimed), he introduced the comedy number, "Bumpity Bump," in which he sang of a wedding, all the attendees at which had wooden legs.[24] The Song would be performed with the use of a cane and the suggestion that one leg was indeed wooden. It was perhaps an unfortunate choice of song in that Askey in old age had both his legs amputated. Life impersonating Art.

There is a telling reference to the legs in commentary from a regional newspaper in 1945:

"Arthur Askey is a miniature wonder on two legs — legs which play their full part in his comedy. The bent knee or the slide and drag of foot beget their own laughter. They are as imperishable in their way as Charlie Chaplin's feet. But Mr. Askey is also master of the crashing witticism and the confidential aside, and can take an ordinary everyday incident and give it a crazy new angle, His industry, also, is something to be seen to be believed."[25]

"Big-Hearted Arthur, That's me," he told the audience. And that is certainly the image that came across the footlights or from television screens, or, for that matter, even if audience could not actually see the comedian, in his radio persona. You liked him from the moment he started to sing what might be considered his theme song:

Big-Hearted Arthur, they call me,
Big-Hearted Arthur, that's me.
Clean if I'm not very clever,
But only 'cause I've got to be.

The title "Big-Hearted" was self-appointed:
"I christened myself. When I was at school and somebody swiped the cricket ball into the next field I would say to the others, 'Never mind. Leave it to Big Hearted Arthur.' And I would go and fetch the ball."[26]

He may have been big-hearted, but Arthur Askey was neither meek nor diffident. "He was not a man of modesty," states Bob Monkhouse,[27] who wrote jokes for him. Unlike some comedians of his generation, he was definitely not always "on" in private life. Debatably, he had a "short fuse" when it came to children, particularly his three grandchildren, and his daughter inherited his fiery temper.[28] Critic/historian Geoff Brown recalls as a child standing in line for Askey's autograph only to be met by a grim-faced comedian who signed every autograph without a smile or a word of greeting. It was required and it was done, but there was no love involved.

June Whitfield disagrees with the assertion that Askey had a different private persona. "Arthur was one of the few comedians who was as funny off screen as he was on, she wrote in her autobiography.[29] In a documentary on the comedian, she insisted, "He was always smiling, and

June Whitfield.

he was a funny man."[30] June Whitfield also claims that Askey was modest, giving as proof that when asked what he was doing at any particular moment, he would respond, "Oh, the usual rubbish."[31]

Her comment in regard to Arthur's always being on is not necessarily a contradictory one. It seems possible that among his peers — his fellow comedians — Askey performed a continuation of his act. When he was with others, there was no need to prove his comedic worth.

With Richard Murdoch, advertising Martini Vermouth.

On *Band Waggon*, Askey's partner, Richard Murdoch, called him "a silly little man," and derogatory as that term might be — although somehow it was always said with affection — it did serve to summarize the comedian's appeal. He was a silly little man, with a silly walk, a silly voice and a silly, infectious laugh. The songs he took delight in were silly. Somehow the lack of height equally seemed a little bit silly.

There was, however, no silliness to the manner in which Askey managed his career. I wonder if he was not the first comedian to embrace commercialism, lending his name and his face to promote products. In July 1939, he and Richard Murdoch signed a one-year contract with Radio Luxembourg to star in a series of thirty-minute shows promoting Symington's Soups. Later, circa 1940, Murdoch and Askey promoted Martini Vermouth, "the Gay Way to Health," thanks to natural aromatic herbs. Askey even made personal appearances promoting the soups as on May 31, 1939, at Coopers Store, Liverpool. World War Two, and the Nazi invasion of Luxembourg, of course, put an end to the longevity of the radio program. In 1947, newspaper readers were being advised that "Arthur Askey sounds better on a new radio from Currys." "Is that Arthur Askey in the Dining Room" asked a 1948 advertisement for Mullard Radios. In 1949, Askey was advertising Ronson lighters in the print media. The December 20, 1949 edition of the *Daily Mirror* contains an advertisement for "Big-Hearted Ronson," with Askey quoted, "Yes, Playmates. It's the slickest lighter I know. And what a wonderful chassis. What beautiful lines. It's a clever little man who can get one of these beauties." In 1953, Arthur was promoting the Ultra Twin Combined Mains and Battery radio. Also in the 1960s, he was to be seen on television commercials for Littlewoods, the Liverpool-based mail order catalog business.

In the summer of 1970, Askey was hired by the Rank Organization Advertising Films Division to star in a one-minute, generic advertising film "Colour in the Home," promoting the sale of color television sets from local retailers.

It may well be that Arthur first realized his potential to sell products while working in *Band Waggon*. Here, he and Richard Murdoch created a fake cleansing powder, Askitoff, made with carbolic acid and turpentine. He was approached by several manufacturers interested in producing such a product, but responded that they would have to wait until the end of the series. Unfortunately for Askey, one company went ahead, registered the name and advertised it as "Britain's Best Cleanser," with a big heart on the label. The whole comic venture actually brought Askey some publicity in America, as *Time* magazine (March 13, 1939) ran a short, one-paragraph piece on Askitoff, describing Arthur as "a sort of British Joe Cook."[32]

Mrs. Askey was also a willing partner in Askey's sales enterprises. In 1940, she joined her husband in promoting the "Big-Hearted Value" of Hercules Cycles.

Not all Askey's promotional activities were commercial in nature. Certainly, during World War Two he worked hard to "stump" on behalf of the War Savings Commission. "Every pound, shilling or penny you put into War Savings you are putting another nail in old Hitler's coffin!" he told an audience in Old Market Square, Nottingham, on September 28, 1940 in a speech the *Nottingham Journal* (September 30, 1940) declared "half sense and half nonsense." A comment that pretty much sums up an Askey performance on stage. A year earlier, in January 1939, Askey had been topping the bill at the Birmingham Hippodrome, appearing on behalf of the Motor and Cycles Trade Benevolent Fund. (Ever understanding of the constant need for publicity, Askey found time, on March 21, 1939, to open a new Kay's Car Park on Birmingham's Bromsgrove Street.) In February 1943, he was topping the bill at the Odeon Theatre, Aylesbury, raising money for the Bucks [Buckinghamshire] Constabulary Widows' and Orphans' Fund.

On the covers of the comic TV Fun.

Unquestionably Arthur Askey understood the value of self-promotion. Beginning in February 1939, he began to contribute a "page of fun," consisting of jokes, quips and fun patter to the national newspaper, the *Sunday Chronicle*. That same year, he was the subject of *Arthur Askey's Annual*. Featuring characters from *Band Waggon*, the annual was published by Oxford University Press at a price of three shillings and six pence. It must be the most entertaining volume ever to come from this lofty academic publisher. The *Annual* was published on September 14, 1939, and advance orders were so exceptionally heavy that the original publication date had to be postponed. While there was only one edition of *Arthur Askey's Annual*, there were other annuals featuring the comedian on the cover: *Radio Fun Annual* 1944 (with Askey front and centre descending on a parachute, along with Tommy Trinder, Flanagan and Allen, and others), *Radio Fun Annual* 1948 (with Askey leading a conga line) and *TV Fun Annual* 1958 (with Askey as a circus ringmaster).

As John Fisher has pointed out it might well be that in the late 1930s, Arthur Askey was the most famous man in the country with the exception of Neville Chamberlain and the royal family.[33]

What Askey failed to do was promote his career much beyond his native Britain. Of his humor, the American trade paper, *Motion Picture Herald*, observed in 1941, "it is one hundred percent British appeal."[34] In April 1947, he took his first vacation in the United States, traveling with his wife and daughter. Also on the trip was his manager, suggesting that an attempt was to be made to interest American promoters in the comedian, but if there was such an approach it failed.

Certainly, around the same time legendary British producer Val Parnell took the opportunity of a U.S. visit to confer with the Shubert Brothers as to the possibility of a British production of the Victor Herbert musical *Sweethearts* as a vehicle for Askey.[35] But nothing came of the idea.

Arthur Askey introduced some of the best-known catchphrases of the first half of the 20th Century, although many of them are perhaps relatively obscure today. In 1941, it was claimed that the greatest catchphrase of the last ten years in Britain was "I Thank You," or as Askey pronounced it, "Ay Thang Yow."[36] The pronunciation, indeed the catchphrase itself, was borrowed from London bus conductors, spoken as they collected their fares. The origin of the catchphrase may have been lost to a modern audience, but it was used by Mike Meyers in the "Austin Powers" films with some success. There were other catchphrases, including "Before Your Very Eyes," "Doesn't It Want to Make You Spit," "Light the Blue Touchpaper and Retire Immediately," and "Hello, Playmates." The last had initially been "Hello Folks," but fellow comedian Tommy Handley complained that it was his catchphrase and Askey presumably agreed.
Later, another pint-sized comedian, Charlie Drake, would use a similar greeting, "Hello, My Darlings."

The catchphrases were given new life as titles for Askey vehicles, such as the 1941 film, *I Thank You*, and the 1941 roadshow, *Hello Playmates*, featuring Mrs. Bagwash's Dancing Daughters taken from *Band Waggon*.

With Richard Murdoch, Askey introduced the catchphrase, "Ah Happy Days," spoken with a wistful sigh, on *Band Waggon* as the two men would reminisce about the past. Similarly, this volume offers a reminiscence of past entertainment, but how wistful will be the response is somewhat questionable in today's culture.

INTRODUCTION 21

1. Wee Georgie Wood (1894-1979) was primarily associated with the variety stage and pantomime; he also wrote a column of commentary on British Music Hall for the trade paper, *The Stage*. I hold a sentimental regard for him in that when I was a teenager I wrote a piece on Old Mother Riley for the *Hull Daily Mail*, and he wrote me a letter praising my work.

2. Jimmy Clitheroe (1921-1973) appeared in variety and pantomime (usually playing Buttons in *Cinderella*), and is generally reported to have been cruel and thoroughly disliked. He died a presumed suicide, after taking an overdose of sleeping tablets, washed down with brandy, on the day of his mother's funeral. He never married and had always lived with his mother.

3. Ronnie Corbett (1930-2016) is best known for his appearances on television and the stage with Ronnie Barker, billed as "The Two Ronnies."

4. Gracie West (1892-1989) usually worked on stage and screen with the tall and lanky Ethel Revnell, billed as "The Long and the Short of It."

5. Harry Relph (1867-1928), a major star of Music Hall and Vaudeville in both the United Kingdom and the United States. Footage of him performing a comic dance titled *Little Tich and His Big Boots* survives and is fairly well known.

6. When Clitheroe tried to transfer his show to television, there was a serious problem in that viewers might be watching an individual of the height of an eleven-yeaer-old child, but the lined and wrinkled face was that of a forty-two-year-old man.

7. Unidentified clipping in Arthur Askey scrapbooks.

8. John Fisher, *Funny Way to be a Hero*, p. 176.

9. Paul Welsh, "Elstree's Contribution to Erotic Cinema History."

10. Eric Midwinter, *Make 'Em Laugh*, p. 54.

11. As reported in the *New York Times* obituary, November 17, 1982.

12. John Martland, "Method in His Madness," p. 11.

13. Russell Harty, *Russell Harty Plus*, p.169.

14. Angela Moreton, "New Little Man Joins Select Club," p. 10.

15. Arthur Askey, "Playmates — I Thank Yeaow," p. 4.

16. Horace Richards, "A Thang Yow!"

17. Jane Stewart to Anthony Slide, e-mail dated February 17, 2020. In an e-mail dated March 12, 2020, she adds, "Both he and mum were furious when the film came out and they saw it in its entirety."

18. Horace Richards, "A Thang Yow!"

19. "Success of Odeon Sunday Concert," p. 5.

20. John Fisher and Tom Atkinson, director, *Comedy Heroes: Arthur Askey*.

21. "Arthur Askey," *The People*, January 8, 1939, p. 11.

22. Arthur Askey, *Before Your Very Eyes*, p. 49.

23. Russell Harty, *Russell Harty Plus*, p. 170.

24. The exact date of the song, indeed even its title, is not known. Presumably, "Bumpity Bump" is taken from the opening line of the chorus to "The Galloping Major," published in 1906.

25. "The Little Man," p. 2.

26. "Arthur Askey Returns to Liverpool," p. 4.

27. John Fisher and Tom Atkinson, director, *Comedy Heroes: Arthur Askey*.

28. William Ewart in conversation with Anthony Slide, November 3, 2018.

29. June Whitfield, *…and June Whitfield*, p. 115.

30. John Fisher and Tom Atkinson, director, *Comedy Heroes: Arthur Askey*.

31. June Whitfield, *…and June* Whitfield, p. 111.

32. Joe Cook (1890-1959) was a major U.S. vaudeville star, who also worked on screen, the legitimate stage and radio.

33. John Fisher, *Funny Way to Be a Hero*, p. 175.

34. *Motion Picture Herald*, March 22, 1941, p. 39.

35. There was currently a Broadway revival of *Sweethearts* that had opened in January 1947, with vaudeville comedian Bobby Clark in the lead.

36. *Motion Picture Herald*, April 19, 1941, p. 30.

Liverpool.

CHAPTER ONE

The Early Years

Liverpool in the North of England may be best known to the world as the birthplace of the Beatles, but it is also the home city of a considerable number of major British comedians, whose names may not be familiar to those outside of the United Kingdom but are or were at one time household names. Among their number are John Bishop, Les Davis, Fred Emney, Deryck Guyler, Tommy Handley, Freddie Starr, Robb Wilton, and Arthur Askey, who, with Ken Dodd, is the finest of all Liverpool's comedy fraternity.

Robb Wilton played one of his better known characters, magistrate Mr. Muddlecombe, opposite Askey on screen in *The Love Match*. And it was Robb Wilton who noted with a certain amount of cynicism, "You've got to have a sense of humour to live around here."

It may not have been a fun place to live, but as one commentator noted, "Merseyside had spawned more major artists than any other area in the country."[1]

As has been recognized, Northern comedians had certain uniform traits. They relied on self-deprecation. They were always ready to prick pomposity. They spoke with a unique English dialogue, identified as "scouse." Just listen to the Beatles in their prime, and you will be hearing the "scouse" dialogue. Above all, Liverpool comedians found the comic in the tragedy of what was, and to a certain extent still is, life in the economically-deprived North of England, an area unkindly described by Southerners as "North of Watford." In other words, a region of the United Kingdom stretching North of the town of Watford, fifteen miles North of London. As Rosemarie Jarski has it, "It is funny up North precisely because it is grim."[2]

In the latter part of the 20th Century, Liverpool was beset with economic problems, poverty and a rising unemployment rate. In the early years of the century, the situation was much different. Liverpool was expanding both in terms of land mass and importance. The shipbuilding industry flourished — the *Titanic* was built there — and Liverpool was often described as the second city of the British Empire. In 1916, the Liver Building, a familiar landmark on the Liverpool skyline opened, and seven years earlier, the city had become home to the first Woolworths in the United Kingdom (perhaps a sign of its working class designation). The city would be forever linked to the slave trade, serving as a major port in the transportation of slaves. Much of its early wealth came from that trade, and, in fact, in December 1999, the city officially apologized for its part in such evil.[3] To Arthur Askey, it was sometimes the subject of humor as he explained he was too young — just — to have been involved.

Liverpool and recognition by its citizens meant a lot to Arthur Askey. When he returned to Liverpool in June 1939 to star at the Empire Theatre, after gaining fame and success in *Band Waggon*, he wrote,

"There are one million of you here on Merseyside, ready to give appreciation to a son of your soil and also ready, I sincerely hope, to judge me on my merits."[4]

He maintained that he had decided not to return to Liverpool until he was earning 250 pounds a week. At his return 250 workers at the Liverpool Municipal Education Department, where he had begun his working life, came to see their former colleague perform at the Empire Theatre.

Ken Dodd

Arthur Askey has acknowledged Ken Dodd as the greatest of all stand-up comedians (which he was) — "for my money, the funniest comedian in the business"[5] — and the two men also have something else in common. Both have made reference in their acts to a mythical race of little people, the Diddy Men, who inhabit Liverpool and are almost as famous as the treacle and jam butty [sandwich] mines of Knotty Ash, a suburb of Liverpool, in which the Diddy Men worked, and to which both men referred.

In 1974, Askey recalled that when he first took his act to London, he was told,

"'We think you're going to be very good, Arthur, but you must drop that Liverpool accent. You must get rid of your accent and you mustn't talk about Diddy men or jam butty factories or treacle mines.' Of course, Ken Dodd comes along thirty-odd years later and, through radio and television, they know what he's talking about. But in those days I was doing missionary work, you know!"[6]

Ken Dodd was born, and died, at 76 Thomas Lane, Knotty Ash, Liverpool. The house was the family home and, apparently, a former farmhouse. Named for his uncle, Arthur Bowden Askey was born in less desirable accommodation at 29 Moses Street, Dingle, on June 6, 1900. The dockland area of Liverpool where the house was located was known as "The Holy Land," with streets named David, Jacob, Isaac, and Moses. His parents, Samuel and Betsy (née Bowden) were working class but upwardly mobile and within six months of Arthur's birth had moved to 90 Rosslyn Street, and later, in 1911, to 58 Sandhurst Street, in the better-class neighborhood of Aigburth.[7] It was a Catholic district of the city (which experienced prejudices similar to those found in Belfast and other Northern Ireland communities), and the Askeys were Methodists, or Wesleyan as they identified themselves, and were subject sometimes to minor acts of violence.

Arthur had a sister, Irene Dorothy, born 1908, known to the family as Rene (pronounced "Reen"). She bore a close resemblance to Arthur and, in later years, would wear trousers which further emphasized the similarity in appearance. A writer for BBC Radio recalls visiting Askey's home and being met at the door by someone whom he assumed to be the comedian in drag — after initially believing he had stumbled upon Arthur's secret life, he discovered the individual was in reality the sister.[8] "Poor girl," wrote Arthur of Rene, "she's so like me, she has to stay indoors when I'm playing Dame in pantomime!"[9]

Arthur's father must have been relatively successful in that his son reported that he was able to retire at the age of fifty-five and live on his investments.

The Askeys were members of the Conservative Party, with the father serving as Honorary Secretary of the local Club. He was an accountant and for much of his working life he was secretary to Sugar Products Company (Liverpool) Limited. Liverpool has something of a reputation for sugar refining in that it is the birthplace of Henry Tate, who started his business there and was later to merge with Abram Lyle and create

LEFT: *Arthur age two.* RIGHT: *Arthur age five and about to start school.*

Tate & Lyle. Mrs. Askey did not work. While Arthur avoided any discussion of politics, it would seem quite clear than, like his father, he was also a supporter of the Conservative Party.

Arthur Askey's childhood was, by all accounts, a very ordinary one. At the age of five he began attending St. Michael's-in-the-Hamlet Primary School. His next-door-neighbor, a Miss Aspinall, taught the young boy to play the piano. With three of his chums, Arthur also attended Professor Dosser's Academy of Dance, located on Lime Street. His social life was centered around the church and he served as a choir boy (eventually becoming head choir boy). "To be a choir boy in those days really meant something," as he pointed out.[10] Construction on the Anglican Liverpool Cathedral began in 1904. When the Lady Chapel, the first part to be completed, was consecrated, on June 29, 1910, Askey was chosen to sing a solo, "Oh for the Wings of a Dove," music by Felix Mendelsohn and lyrics by William Bartholomew, and to participate in a quartet, "God Is a Spirit" by William Sterndale Bennett. The performance at Liverpool Cathedral might well be designated Arthur Askey's first public appearance even if the stage was simply the choir stall of the Cathedral.

"As a kid there was always music in the house," reminisced Arthur in 1977, "and by the age of seven I had started to learn the piano. Then, of

Sister Rene, with compere Eamon Andrews and Askey's wife May on This Is Your Life.

course, I joined the church choir and spent a lot of my early life taking part in church concerts and Sunday singing.

"I remember when the choirmaster gave me permission, I used to have a go on the church organ. It was a three manual organ and I remember having difficulty reaching the pedals because my legs were so short. Of course, they're not that much longer now.

"I like the melodious classics. I'm not really fond of Bach."[11]

During the season, Arthur and his father were regularly in the stands watching Everton Football Club play. Indeed, two of the Askey family's neighbors, Jack Sharp and Harry Makepeace, were Everton players. Everton is one of two football clubs in Liverpool, with the other being Liverpool City, and there was and is fierce rivalry between the two.[12] (In later years, Arthur was a massive fan of West Ham United Football Club, based in Stratford, East London.)

In 1911, the young Askey became a paying pupil at the Liverpool Institute for Boys, spending six years there. Apparently, he sat at the same desk later occupied by Paul McCartney, who, along with George Harrison, is an old boy of the Institute. As Askey recalled,

"I loved my six years at 'Inny.' I was no great scholar, but I did enjoy history and geography. Ordinary maths I could cope with, but algebra beat me and still does.…I played cricket and football for the school."[13]

Askey became the school and choir comic. As he admitted, he would usually be chosen for the football and cricket teams because he made his fellow players laugh on the train journeying to away matches.

The Liverpool Institute was the equivalent of a grammar school, a British high school catering to boys from eleven through eighteen of more than average intelligence. Those designated less intelligent attended a comprehensive school. In 1985, a left-wing Labor Council in Liverpool closed the school, but in 1996, under the aegis of Paul McCartney, the school reopened as the Liverpool Institute for Performing Arts.

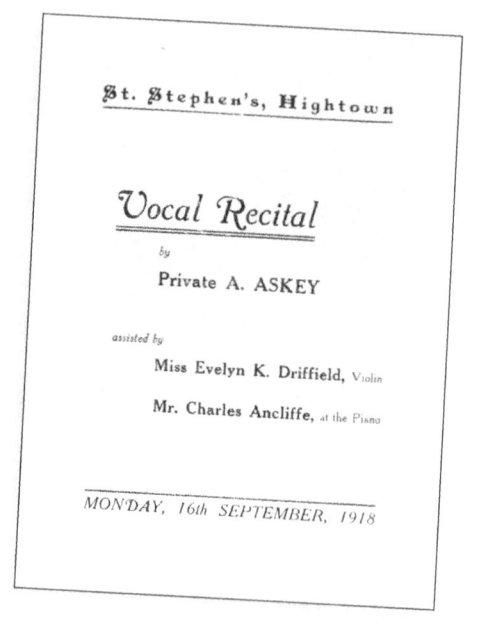

> St. Stephen's, Hightown
>
> *Vocal Recital*
> by
> Private A. ASKEY
>
> assisted by
>
> Miss Evelyn K. Driffield, Violin
>
> Mr. Charles Ancliffe, at the Piano
>
> MONDAY, 16th SEPTEMBER, 1918

When Askey graduated in 1916, there were few opportunities for boys such as himself, with an average education but no special, discernible talents. Like many similar grammar school graduates, including this writer, the only job opportunity available was with the local council. He worked as a clerk in the Municipal Education Department, in what he termed the "Tonsils and Adenoids Department." Its primary function was to make appointments for children to have their tonsils and/or adenoids removed.

Askey was to leave local government for a career in show business, which did not exactly please his father who thought the son should have stayed with the Municipal Education Department for the remainder of his working life and received an appropriate pension. One of his colleagues, Frank Ball, recalled,

"Arthur played football for the office team and once gave a perfect pass off his backside to the wingman without using his feet. On his last day in the office he brought several bottles of port for a farewell toast. Some of us had doubts about whether he was doing the right thing in leaving to join a concert party."[14]

World War One intervened in Askey's career in local government, and in 1918, at the age of eighteen he was called up — and despite his height and his short-sightedness, he was found fully equipped to serve his country with the Welsh Infantry Regiment. The service was brief. It began on June 6, 1918, and on November 11 of that year, peace was formally declared. Arthur had not left the country during his military service, and because he was working in local government, in a job considered "pivotal" to the war or rather the peace effort, he was discharged concurrent with the formal end of hostilities.

1. Geoff Leack, "Merseyside — Cradle of Show Business Talent," p. 177.

2. Rosemarie Jarski, *The Wit and Wisdom of the North.*

3. Liverpool is home to the International Slavery Museum, opened in 2007, and located on the city's Albert Dock (now a World Heritage site).

4. Arthur Askey, "Playmates — I Thank Yeaow!," p. 4.

5. Arthur Askey, *Before Your Very Eyes,* p. 41.

6. Russell Harty, *Russell Harty Plus,* p. 169.

7. 58 Sandhurst Street sold in 2015 for 151,500 pounds (the equivalent of $208,000.00). In 2018, a furnished room was available for rent at 29 Moses Street for 65 pounds a week (the equivalent of $89.00).

8. Michael Pointon in conversation with Anthony Slide, October 31, 2018.

9. Arthur Askey, *Before Your Very Eyes,* p. 179.

10. *Desert Island Discs,* December 26, 1980.

11. "Arthur Askey — Diminutive Giant,"p. 7.

12. The Liverpool City club anthem is Rodgers and Hammerstein's "You'll Never Walk Alone."

13. Arthur Askey, *Before Your Very Eyes,* p. 22.

14. Horace Richards, "Ay Thang Yow!"

Arthur's first professional photograph.

CHAPTER TWO

The Beginnings of a Show Business Career

The Askey family would spend its two-week summer vacation in the North Wales resort of Rhyl, a popular holiday spot for working class families from Liverpool and Manchester. The connection between Liverpool and North Wales was such that the city, despite being in England, was often described as the capital of that part of Wales. In the 1970s, Rhyl lost two of what must have been to Askey its best-known landmarks, the pier and the Pavilion Theatre. Once an affluent community, Rhyl has gradually deteriorated through the years, and in 2017, it was ranked top of the list of the Ten Worst Places to live in Wales. But to Askey, it was the BBC of seaside resorts — Bingo, Beer and Chips!

In the 1910s and the decades that followed, a staple of entertainment in seaside resorts such as Rhyl were the concert parties on the beach itself or, more likely, in a theatre at the end of the pier. These concert parties consisted of a small group of entertainers, who would sing, dance and tell jokes, usually dressed in loose-fitting identical costumes. The "artistes," as they liked to call themselves were multi-talented and generally could take any part. In that the early concert parties were all-male, one such part would be that of the female. J.B. Priestley used a concert party, "The Dinky Doos," for the background in his 1929 novel, *The Good Companions*, which has been adapted a number of times for screen and stage.

In Rhyl, the young Arthur became entranced with a concert party known as the "Jovial Jesters," and operated by a man named Gilbert Rogers. The company was all-male with one of its number, Cecil Barnard, working as a female impersonator with the name of Phoebe.[1] Beginning in 1906, the group had performed three times a day, at 11:00, 3:00 and 7:00, on a wooden platform set up on the sands, with a member of the troupe required to go through the audience with a collecting box in lieu of paid tickets. Arthur recalled later that he would sometimes be selected to persuade the audience to pay and he was told, "If someone is asleep in a deckchair, rattle the box to wake him."[2] At virtually every performance, the young Askey would be seated as close to the raised stage as possible with a penny provided by his father to contribute to the box office. "I knew all their songs, all their jokes," remembered Askey. "I'm still cracking a few of them."

On June 2, 1914, the *Birmingham Mail* reported, "Mr. Gilbert Rogers and his Jovial Jesters have opened well on the sands where close by Madame Hengler had a troupe of performing dogs. With three picture palaces going, Rhyl had no dearth of entertainments."

Askey learned the songs and sketches by heart, and wrote many years later, "I think that I can honestly say the 'Jovial Jesters' gave me the bug for show business.'"[3]

The comedian returned to Rhyl in the summer of 1964, topping the bill at the city's Pavilion Theatre.

Obviously, Arthur Askey had always wanted to entertain in some fashion, and his parents accepted this by sending him both for piano and dance lessons. "When I was little I used to give performances with my sister's dolls and teddy bears as the audience," he recalled in 1939.[4] Reminiscing in much later years, Askey commented,

"Someone would bring along a violin, someone else would play the piano, someone would crack a few jokes — we'd make our own fun. There were always also a lot of church concerts always being put on, and everyone had the chance to be an entertainer. It's not like that nowadays, unfortunately. People mostly want to be entertained, rather than entertain themselves."[5]

Prior to military service, while a teenager, Askey had entertained wounded soldiers, singing sentimental ballads and later comic songs, often performing as a duo with Tommy Handley, who was to become Britain's first great radio comedian. Handley would sing "The Road to Mandalay." Askey would sing "Roses of Picardy." And then the two would combine their talents on "The Two Gendarmes," with music by Jacques Offenbach. Also known as "The Bold Gendarmes, the chorus explains the facetiousness of the title:

But when we meet a helpless woman
Or little boys who do no harm,
We run them in, we run them in,
We show them we're the bold gendarmes.

As Askey explained, his entertainment of the troops "suited me for two good reasons. It meant afternoons off from school every week and plenty of free tea parties.

"Then my voice broke and things looked pretty black! Now that I couldn't sing ballads any more my holidays and tea parties ended.

"But I had a brainwave. I learned a couple of comic songs and blossomed out as a youthful comedian.

"In a week or two they were marking little Arthur Askey 'Absent' again, and I was back trying to make the soldiers laugh, and eating more free teas than were good for me!"[6]

During the brief time he was in the army, Askey would play the piano for the weekly dances in the Sergeants' Mess. He also performed as a serious singer, and a program is extant of what must have been a typical show, in which Private Arthur Askey sings twelve numbers, ranging from "The Floral Dance" and "The Gentle Maiden" to the prologue from *Pagliacci* and "The Toreador's Song" from Bizet's *Carmen*.

The Filberts

In Liverpool, in 1921, he established his own concert party, "The Filberts" with its members dressed in pierrot-like costumes, performing in church halls, hospitals and the like. (A filbert is a type of hazelnut, and so the name obviously identifies the members of the group as being nuts.)

Arthur also worked with another concert party, "The Scarletts," playing the piano. A brief visit to London trying to obtain professional employment proved abortive, and a somewhat disillusioned Arthur Askey returned to Liverpool and his job with the Education Office. He also became engaged to Elizabeth May Swash, a shorthand-typist with Goodlass Walls, a paint manufacturer that remains active to the present. The couple married on March 23, 1925.

For the first couple of years of the marriage, May traveled with her husband, appearing as a singer/dancer with the concert party. She was not, however, someone who felt comfortable with a life in the public eye, and kept firmly divorced from her husband's career. She didn't disapprove, she was simply disinterested. Askey once commented,

"I always used to say that she thought I was a burglar. She knew I went out at night to do something, but she wasn't quite sure what it was....She was most untheatrical. If I mentioned So-and-So — Danny Kaye, for instance — she'd say, 'Who's that?'"[7]

At this time, Askey's act was basically second-hand. As he recalled,

"I was very much thieved. I used to go to the local music hall and listen to the comedian and if I heard a funny joke I would take it. But I didn't do that for long. One of the first things I learned as a professional was that I had to be original. I had to be a bit different from the others, and not use other people's material. Fortunately I discovered I could write gags and patter and songs to suit my act."[8]

The Filberts came to the attention of a columnist in the local newspaper, the *Liverpool Echo*, in 1923, and under the headline, "Ask(ey)ing for It," he wrote,

"A colleague, who has seen all the local concert parties at one time or another, tells me that Arthur Askey, the funny man of the 'Filberts,' is far and away the best amateur comedian on Merseyside. He compares favorably with many of the pros., and should he ever think of making it a whole-time he feels sure he would soon be snapped up."[9]

Outside of the summer season, Askey would keep busy. For example, on November 10, 1923, he sang a humorous song, "Househunting," at the 5th Annual Reunion of Ex-Service Men, held at the Washington Hotel, Liverpool.

In pierrot costume for "The Filberts".

That same year, Askey learned of a professional concert in need of a new comedian. The concert party was called "Song Salad," under the management of George Beachcroft and Martin Newman. On March 16, 1924, Askew took the train from Liverpool's Lime Street Station to London Euston, ready to begin rehearsals in Brixton for an opening beginning on March 31 at the Headgate Electric Theatre, which, since 1910, had primarily operated as a movie theatre, in Colchester, Essex.[10] From Colchester, the company moved on to Ventnor, Southsea, Plymouth, London (the Crystal Palace), Liverpool, Limerick (Ireland),

Cork (Ireland), Rock Ferry, Rhyl, Cardiff, Glasgow, Hereford, Ilfracombe, Bedford, Weymouth, Worthing, Brighton, Taunton, Torquay, Exmouth, Morecambe, and Dalton-in-Furness, where the tour ended.

The humor consisted of gags such as:

"Do you know 'The Road to Mandalay'?"
"Yes, do you want me to sing it?"
"No — take it."[11]

While in Weymouth, at the Alexandria Gardens, on August 11, 1924, Askey made his first radio broadcast in company with George Beachcroft and Margot Domican (who sang a duet). A second broadcast, also from Weymouth, took place on September 23, 1925. Also, as a result of his work in "Song Salad," Arthur was given a contract for his first professional appearance in pantomime, *Little Miss Muffet*, for three weeks at the South Parade Pier, Southsea, and six weeks on tour. For his work, Askey recalled that he was paid twelve pounds a week, almost double his salary in "Song Salad." He was required to provide his own costume, with the help of his wife, mother and sister, and he wore a red wig with a center parting and a bun, based on one Askey had seen George Robey wear in pantomime.

A ditty that he introduced in Southsea began,

"I love Southsea in the summer,
Southsea's always gay and bright.
But I love Southsea when it's raining.
We get full houses every night."

As he would explain "I always take my holidays early in the season — before the sheets [in the boarding houses] get too dirty."

Around this time, Arthur came to the attention of Clarkson Rose, a legendary concert party producer and comedian. Looking back in the 1930s, he described Askey as a cross between comedian Leslie Henson and musical comedy star Bobby Howes:

"Arthur is the best all round comic in concert party today. He has every asset a comedian should have of his type, dapper, diminutive, smart and alert, and, above all, full of resource. Add to these a pleasant voice, an ability to trip a measure and play the piano, and you have the complete box of tricks."[12]

Many years later, Askey paid tribute to his time in concert parties with a recording of "The Seaside Band," a fast-paced little number, performed on screen to the disgust of his fellow stranded passengers in *The Ghost Train*.[13] The opening verse reads:

Once, at the seaside, feeling very restless
I ran down tuppence and I rolled on the pier.
Hadn't gone far when the strains of music
Floated on the breeze and landed in my ear.
I quickened up my steps for I love nice noises.
Very soon arrived right opposite the band.
Saw the conductor on a lemonade box,
With his little baton stuck up in his right hand.

Six more verses followed.

Kenneth Blain

"The Seaside Band" was written by Askey, with music by Kenneth Blain. The latter has never received much credit for his work as the composer of this song and also "The Moth," featured in *Miss London Ltd* and "A Pretty Bird," featured in *Band Waggon*. Most importantly, it was Kenneth Blain who wrote both the music and the lyrics for "The Bee Song."

Very little is known about the composer, but Blain appears to have been born, like Askey, in Liverpool and he also had his own variety act in which he would perform songs closely associated with Arthur. Askey recalls that he first met Blain when he was working at London's Windmill Theatre in the 1930s. Blain told Arthur of the song he had written that he thought would suit him — and it did. For the privilege of performing "The Bee Song," Askey would pay Blain two guineas (or two pounds and two shillings) a performance. One gets the impression that Arthur never fully appreciated Kenneth Blain and his talent; certainly in later years he would often not bother to mention Blane's name as the composer of the songs. "Kenneth made quite a bid of money out of it, apart from what I paid him through the years. But he resented the fact that *he* couldn't get it over in his performance all the same. He was a fine writer, almost in the Gilbert and Sullivan class."[14] I believe that Kenneth Blain is the uncredited pianist who appears with Askey as he sings "The Bee Song" in a 1937 *Pathe Pictorial*.

When Kenneth Blain ran out of inspiration, Arthur would write similar songs himself, such as "The Seagull," "The Worm" and "The Mosquito." "The Worm" sadly foreshadows that happened to Arthur in old age:

*"When I was out wriggling through the dew
The Farmer's spade cut me in two.
I felt so silly; it made me laugh,
Saying good night to my better half."*

In the early 1930s, Askey also acquired at least one song, "I've Got Nothing Much to Do," from Percival Langley. But none could compare with "The Bee Song."

In 1925, Arthur continued his work in "Song Salad," joined by his new bride, May, who was booked as the soprano. And that Christmas, he was again in pantomime, this time at the Theatre Royal, Torquay, playing Buttons in *Babes in the Wood*. Askey recalled a good review he received in the local newspaper:

"Arthur Askey as 'Buttons' is immensely amusing. One would like to see him afforded even greater chances for attacking the risible faculties because there seemed to a reserve of power and talent behind everything he did, which was not called into full play."[15]

Following the Christmas and early New Year weeks at the Lyceum Theatre, Torquay, *Babes in the Wood* went on a tour. Askey's weekly salary was eight pounds.[16] Reviews here were again positive, with the *Taunton Courier and Western Advertiser* (January 27, 1926) commenting, "Arthur Askey…is a number quite on his own, and can always be relied upon to produce a convulsive roar of laugher."

Early Contracts

Extant contracts are evidence of Askey's quickly rising pay checks and of his popularity. His earliest theatrical contract is with Messrs. Newman & Beachcroft for *Song Salad*. Dated March 1, 1924, it is for a tour beginning March 31, 1924, at six pounds, ten shillings a week. A second contract for both Askey and wife, May, with the same producers is dated September 1924, for a tour beginning Easter 1925 at ten pounds, ten shillings per week.

In April 1926, he signed with Fred Clement's Pantomime Productions Limited as "A Comedian (and understudy if necessary)" at eleven pounds a week. His wife, May Bowden, signed at the same time as "A Chorus Lady (and understudy if necessary)" at three pounds per week. The following year, a contract dated January 1927, assured Askey of twelve pounds a week as "A Principal" in pantomime, beginning December 26, 1927. A contract with Fred Clement's Pantomime Productions Limited, dated December 26, 1928, has Askey paid fourteen pounds a week as "A Principal Comedian." On May 10, 1926, he signed a contract with Fred Wilson's Margate Entertainers for the period May 22 through October 9 of that year at a weekly salary of twelve pounds.

On September 18, 1929, Askey signed with Powis Pinder's Sunshine Company for the 1930 Shanklin Season at eighteen pounds a week, plus twenty-five percent of any benefit performances. A contract dated September 22, 1931, guaranteed Askey twenty pounds a week for the 1932 Summer Season at Shanklin, and a contract dated August 26, 1933, promised him twenty-four pounds for the 1934 season. He signed with Powis Pinder on August 26, 1934, for the 1935 Summer Season in Shanklin, at a weekly salary of twenty-six pounds a week. Again with Powis Pinder, a contract dated August 6, 1935, for the Shanklin Summer Season next year was at a weekly salary of thirty pounds a week.

The last contract that Arthur Askey kept is with Greatrex Newman (London). Dated October 13, 1937, it guarantees him forty pounds a week for an unspecified period.

To a large extent, Arthur Askey's career had adopted a familiar course. It might even be claimed that he was in a rut, with pantomime in the winter and concert parties in the summer. He was no longer with "Song Salad," but in 1926, he had joined Fred Wildon's Entertainers [17] in Margate, giving two performances a day at 3:00 and 7:00 p.m. Askey also discovered the financial joys of entertaining after formal dinners at Masonic lodges and elsewhere. By the 1930s, the comedian was featured at various night spots in London, ranging from the Connaught Rooms and the Savoy Hotel to Frascati's and the Café de Paris. He appeared at the Cosmo Club on Wardour Street in London's Soho, and had a brief and disappointing, one-night engagement at Herbert Henri's Chez Henri on Long Acre. Askey was obviously too unsophisticated for this nightspot, which had featured American-born pianist Charlie Kunz for some eight-and-a-half years, and was also a long-time venue for Leslie "Hutch" Hutchinson, a black pianist and singer who enjoyed a long, sexual relationship with Lord Louis Mountbatten's wife, Edwina.[18]

Askey also appeared at what might well be considered lesser events. For example, on January 30, 1930, *The Stage* reported that the comedian had entertained the staff at the annual dinner of Frederick Sage, Ltd. at the Holborn Restaurant.

As early as March 19, 1931, *The Stage* hailed Askey as a "popular laughtermaker," when he entertained a fraternal group identified as The Owls at London's Cannon Street Hotel.

He worked with Fred Wildon in Margate through 1929, and the readers of the *Daily Mail* voted Askey as their favorite Seaside Comedian. As a result, he received at least one review, in the *Daily Mail* of course, whose critic, William Pollock, was not overly generous in his praise:

"Mr. Arthur Askey is a very short man with red hair and a pair of very large horn-rimmed spectacles...."

With Fred Wildon's Margate Entertainers; Arthur is top row, far right.

"For the last fortnight postcards have poured in from readers of The Daily Mail resident or holiday-making at a certain specified South of England seaside town recommending the merits or this and that concert party comedian or comedienne. Mr. Askey's name has been on a great many of them.

"Well, to-day I have watched Mr. Askey. He showed symptoms of being able to amuse in a way of his own. Physically he reminded me of Mr. Nelson Keys;[19] in methods he is not so glitteringly definite and clear-cut. He is slower and his face face is not so classic.

"I thought his material was poor, but that he handled it with assurance and with a voice that carries well. He did not dance, but he looks as if he could.

"At present I should not put Mr. Askey down as being ready to step into a leading part on the West End stage, but he is a young man with possibilities."[20]

It is an interesting review in large part because it does suggest what Askey's act was to continue to be and what it was to become. He did project well. He could dance, and dancing around the stage became a major part of his act. He could barely keep still. And "the symptoms of being able to amuse" were obviously there from his teenage years and were to become full blown within a few years. Rather like Noel Coward, Arthur Askey might be said to have "A Talent to Amuse."

Askey's stage career (particularly in pantomime) prospered, as discussed in Chapter Five. On October 8, 1933, he appeared at the Lewisham Town Hall, with comediennes Elsie and Doris Waters. On October 22 of the same year, he was at London's Finsbury Park Empire with the venerable stage actor, Seymour Hicks.

Also in 1933, Askey introduced the comic song with which he is most associated, "The Bee," five verses long, with its once famous opening lines,

Oh what a wonderful thing to be,
a healthy, grown-up, busy, busy bee,
Whiling away all the passing hours
Pinching all the pollen from the cauliflowers.

Two years later, in 1935, Askey introduced a monologue titled "All to Specification," written by Robert Rutherford and Frank Wilcox. Unknown today and seldom referenced in regard to the comedian, "All to Specification" was once a big hit with audiences:

For months and months I searched both near and far
To find a house — you know how scarce they are:
But glory be, I got one t'other day.
I bought it from an agent who was giving it away:
Five thousand pounds — that's all, just as it stands —
Two bedrooms and a place to wash your hands.

Through five more verses, the problems with the house are recorded, each ending with the pronouncement, "And it's — all to specification."

The monologue ends:

"The gable-end fell down today and messed things up a bit,
A bricklayer came round — he said, "I know the cause of it —
Them bricks ain't got no mortar on — they've stuck 'em up with spit!"
There's no place like home, and it's — all to specification.

As late as 1950, Arthur and daughter Anthea were introducing animal-related songs, such as "Every Little Piggy's Got a Curly tail," written by Guy Dearden, recorded on H.M.V.. It was promoted as "The biggest chorus song for years."

In 1929, Arthur was hired by the BBC to participate in what were called "Empire Broadcasts," broadcast live to the outreaches of the British Empire, Australia, New Zealand, Canada, and elsewhere. On January 14, 1936, the BBC's Empire Service broadcast a mid-day program, from 12:15 through 1:00 p.m. titled *Shiver Me Timbers or the Irate Pirate*. Arthur Askey was both the star and the writer. In February 1931, Askey was back on radio in *John Sharman's Music Hall*. The program was a staple of Saturday night entertainment on the BBC, with its theme song, "The Spice of Life." The comedian was also featured in the BBC's National Variety shows; for example, on October 9, 1933, he co-starred with Michael Hogan, Mabel Constanduras and the Seven Singing Sisters. Askey was later to be heard as the character of Able Seaman Nobby Clarke, with Jack Barty and Fred Gwyn, in an occasional BBC series, *Eight Bells*, with a Naval theme, first heard in April 1935.[21] *Eight Bells* was revived as *Eight Bells Home Again* in January 1946, but without Askey. In 1937, Askey made his screen debut, such as it was, in *Calling All Stars*.

Powis Pinder's Sunshine Company

From summer months in Margate, the comedian had moved on to summer months in Shanklin, on the Isle of Wight, with Powis "Poppa" Pinder's Sunshine Company,[22] with whom he appeared for some eight years.

While Askey was appearing in Shanklin, another young boy had taken to going at least three times a week to watch the comedian's performance. Years later, that young boy told Askey, "You looked so happy and carefree up there....I owe the fact that I went on the stage to you." The young boy was actor David Niven.

There were major changes in Arthur Askey's family life. Or at least one prominent change, and that was an addition to the family of a daughter, Anthea Shirley, born on March 2, 1933. The name "Anthea" was chosen because of a song, "To Anthea," inspired by poet Ben Jonson, and sung by Webster Booth as a member of the Sunshine Company. The entire Sunshine Company was present at Anthea's christening in Shanklin on July 30, 1933. Three years later, the family moved to a larger apartment in the North London suburb of Golders Green. The Askeys also boasted of owning a car and a maid. "I had mentally settled down to a routine of concert party and concerts and was feeling very pleased with life," Askey recalled in later years.[23]

There was no particular reason for Arthur to believe that life might change for him — least of all for the better — but it did, and it was all thanks to the BBC.

Anthea Askey in Ramsbottom Rides Again.

1. Cecil Bernard was relatively well-known in the North of England as a vocalist and female impersonator, playing the dame in pantomime. As late as 1942, he played Dame Durdon in *Babes in the Wood* at the Hippodrome, Bury.

2. John Vose, "Big-Hearted Arthur."

3. Arthur Askey, *Before Your Very Eyes*, p. 20.

4. "Arthur Askey Returns to Liverpool," p. 4

5. Quoted in *The Stage*, January 31, 1980, p. 177.

6. "Meet Big Hearted Arthur," p. 11.

7. Russell Harty, *Russell Harty Plus*, p. 170.

8. Unsourced clipping in one of Arthur Askey's scrapbooks.

9. Reprinted in the *Liverpool Echo*, September 5, 1941, p. 4. I have been unable to locate the exact date of original publication.

10. A plaque was later placed on the theatre frontage, reading, "In this building opened in 1910 as the Headgate Electric Theatre ARTHUR ASKEY C.B.E. COMEDIAN made his first professional appearance 31st March 1924."

11. The popularity of "The Road to Mandalay" in British comedy routines is quite remarkable, and, of course, no Ken Dodd performance would be complete without his slapstick rendition of Rudyard Kipling's classic 1890 ode.

12. Clarkson Rose, "Peradventure," p. 2. Clarkson Rose (1890-1968) headed a concert party titled "Twinkle," along with his wife, Olive Fox. It began on Ryde Pier in 1921 and continued for forty-seven years, from 1935 onwards at the Eastbourne Pier Pavilion

13. Recorded May 21, 1952 on Decca F.9944.

14. Arthur Askey, *Before Your Very Eyes*, p. 79.

15. Ibid, p. 54. I have been unable to find the source of this review.

16. Contract dated December 26, 1925.

17. Fred Wildon was earlier known as "The Musical Golliwog," dressed as the racially offensive doll and performing as a one-man band.

18. It is delightful to report that Hutch (1900-1969) also had relationships with Cole Porter, Tallulah Bankhead, Ivor Novello, and Merle Oberon.

19. Nelson Keys (1886-1939) was a British star of musical comedy and revue, who also worked in the United States.

20. Arthur Askey, *Before Your Very Eyes*, p. 64.

21. *Eight Bells* also featured Fred Gwyn, John Rorke and Fred Yule. It was produced by Harry S. Popper. The series was revived in January 1946 under the title of *Eight Bells Home Again*.

22. Powis Pinder (1872-1941) was for many years, between 1894 and 1903, a member of the D'Oyly Carte Opera Company.

23. Arthur Askey, *Before Your Very Eyes*, p. 82.

Arthur in fine form broadcasting to his radio audience.

CHAPTER THREE

Band Waggon

To celebrate the coronation of King George VI the BBC on May 11, 1937 presented a major variety show on radio titled *The Coronation Review*. The BBC also broadcast the coronation itself live the following day; it was the first coronation to be broadcast live on both radio and television, and the first to be filmed. Just as the Coronation marked the end of an era and the beginning of a new one for the monarchy, it may also be said to have marked the beginning of a new era in entertainment for Arthur Askey. Yes, the comedian had been heard on radio since the 1920s, but this was a major broadcast — the most important of the year if not the decade — honoring a new king.

Askey was one of a multitude of featured stars, including Cicely Courtneidge, Frank Lawton, Harry Welchman, the Western Brothers, Mabel Costanduras, Reginald Foort, "Hutch," and Ethel Revnell and Gracie West. Max Miller was originally to have been the master of ceremonies along with veteran and legendary British comedian George Robey, but he proved incapable of reading spontaneously from a script, and Askey was asked to replace him. It soon became apparent that Robey was going to steal the limelight and the best jokes from Askey. In retaliation, on the night, Askey began to ad-lib and completely stole the show from Robey.

John Watt

When Askey was called in the next day to meet with the BBC's director of variety, John Watt, he thought he was to be reprimanded. Instead, he was asked if he would be interested in performing in an American-style comedy series which would be broadcast at the same day and time each week.

As he recalled for John Watt's widow,

"Some weeks later John, in search of a resident comedian for the comedy show he was thinking of doing (he didn't want an established radio comic like Tommy Handley or Leonard Henry) arranged to meet two comedians in two different pubs. He flipped a coin to decide which pub to choose. He went to the one where Arthur was waiting. 'As far as I know, the other chap is still waiting...And thanks to John, I got my big chance which made me the biggest name in radio, and from which came West-End shows, films, television, Music Hall and a smile on the face of my bank manager."[1]

And thus are legends made. Although it must be noted that other sources claim that Tommy Trinder was initially cast in the lead, but when he became unavailable, Askey was the second choice.[2] Leonard Henry (1890-1973) was once one of the most popular radio comedians of the 1930s, noted for his ability to create jokes from subjects suggested by his audience. He is largely forgotten today. Tommy Handley (1892-1949) was to star in the successor to *Band Waggon*, *It's That Man Again* or *ITMA*, which was heard on BBC radio from 1939 through 1949, and only ended with the death of its star. Replacing *ITMA*, in turn, as the most popular BBC radio program of the era was *Take It from Here* with Jimmy Edwards, Dick Bentley and Joy Nichols.

John Watt (1901-1960) was responsible not only for *Band Waggon* and *ITMA* but also *Workers' Playtime*, featuring popular music of the day. He had succeeded Eric Maschwitz at the BBC; in later years, from 1950-1951, Watt was compere of the request program, *Housewives Choice*, and was married to novelist Angela (Violette) Jeans.

American comedian Jack Benny was identified as a radio performer whose show influenced *Band Waggon*. And Askey, himself, claimed to have been influence by Benny. "The tendency on this side of the Atlantic is for characters to be eccentric, even grotesque. Jack Benny, whatever strange happenings he lets himself in for, is himself and nobody else."[3]

The initial concept for *Band Waggon* was to have a compere and a resident comedian introducing and inserting comedic interludes between dance numbers (provided by the Bandwaggoners conducted by Phil Cardew and with songs by the Jackdaws), and organ recitals (by Reginald Foort and later Charles Smart at the BBC Theatre Organ).

Richard Murdoch

For the compere, the BBC hired Richard Murdoch (1907-1990); he replaced Freddie Birtwell who was to have been the original straight man opposite Askey. In many respects, Murdoch was the antithesis of Arthur Askey. He had been educated at Pembroke College, Cambridge after attending Charterhouse public school. Because of his upbringing,

Murdoch was nicknamed "Stinker" on *Band Waggon*, while Arthur for obvious reasons became "Big." Richard Murdooch was tall, of athletic build, with relatively good looks and a very superior accent. His screen career dated back to 1932, and it ended, with his performance as Uncle Tom in the BBC series, *Rumpole of the Bailey* from 1978-1991. He had made his West End stage debut in 1930 in one of C.B. Cochran's *Reviews*.

LEFT: *John Watt.* RIGHT: *Richard Murdoch.*

Richard Murdoch served with distinction during World War Two with the R.A.F., and after the war he had returned to radio to co-star with Kenneth Horne in the immensely popular *Much Binding in the Marsh*. From 1962 through 1977, he played one of two incompetent civil servants on the long-running BBC radio series, *The Men from the Ministery*.

Askey and Murdoch worked on the scripts for *Band Waggon* along with credited writers Gordon Crier and Vernon Harris. The series was co-produced by Gordon Crier and Vernon Harris, with Penny Worth assisting. Askey was in every way the BBC's resident comedian, with the sketches involving the couple sharing a top floor flat at Broadcasting House, where they were joined by Lewis the Goat, pigeons Basil, Lucy, Ronald, and Sarah. "A goat in the flat — what about the smell? Oh, he'll get used to it." At one point, a camel named Hector had been added to the menagerie, but his presence was considered too silly to contemplate.

The other two human members of the cast were charwoman (or household cleaner) Mrs. Bagwash and her daughter, Nausea, neither of whom actually spoke to the radio audience. Mrs. Bagwash would occasionally grunt while Nausea would always faint when confronted by the microphone. The ongoing plot in part involved Arthur's lack of success in courting Nausea. In a classic sketch, "The Proposal," Richard Murdoch demonstrates to Askey how he might propose to his beloved. The sketch was first heard on November 23, 1938, and a later performance for the troops was issued as a gramophone recording.

Broadcasting House adorned with the images of Askey and Murdoch.

When bathroom facilities were needed, Askey and Murdoch used those of the BBC announcers on the floor below. To boil eggs for breakfast, a kettle would be lowered, by way of a string, onto the fireplace of BBC Director General Lord Reith. For soft-boiled eggs, the pair would sing one chorus of "Hands, Knees and Boomps-a-Daisy." For hard-boiled, two choruses would be required. It is claimed that the reference to the BBC as "Auntie" was first used on *Band Waggon*.

Askey and Murdoch at the height of their fame.

Providing laughs were various special sound effects, presented by a sound effects man who would often dress for the part, much annoying Askey, who yelled, "Oi! I'm the comedian." Additionally, *Band Waggon* was the first show to make use of catchphrases on a regular basis, such as "Doesn't It Want to Make You Spit," "Don't Be Filthy," and "Light the blue touchpaper and retire immediately," when withdrawing from a confrontation with Mrs. Bagwash. It was the latter who was responsible for the longest catchphrase in radio history. In response to "Who's she?" came the answer, "The woman who's come to do the spring cleaning." "She's very quiet isn't she?" "Ah, it isn't the people who make the most noise who do the most work."

The show also boasted various special features. There was "New Voices," which introduced Vanessa Lee who was to become a leading lady in Ivor Novello musicals. Comedian Siyd Walker appeared as "Mr. Walker Wants to Know," playing that unique British institution, a rag-and-bone man who would go around the streets of the community, with a horse-drawn wagon, collecting unwanted household goods. Old gags were recycled under the heading of chestnut corner. German-born Hans Wolfgang Priwin, who had created and written the Inspector Hornleigh mysteries on radio from 1937-1940 and also the screen adaptations starring Gordon Harker, hosted a radio mystery puzzle, "What Do You Think".

As befitted his stature as star of the show, Askey was given a solo spot, introduced by the song "Big Hearted Arthur, They Call Me." He would present parodies of popular songs and read letters he had received, such as:

"Dear Mr. Askey, we understand that when you were a child your Uncle Aubrey offered you $100.00 if you would give up your idea of becoming a comedian. We should be glad if you will advise us as to how you spent the money. Yours regretfully, the BBC."

Askey and Murdoch were themselves on the show, and audiences actually believed in them and the flat. Hundreds of letters were received each week, sent to the flat's make-believe address.

As John Fisher has written,

"For a while Arthur may well have been the most famous man in the country after Neville Chamberlain and the royal family...Between December 1938 and March 1939, a crucial time in British political history, listening figures reveal that the show attracted a larger percentage of the potential audience than the six o'clock news. When the show was about to return a month after the outbreak of war, the chancellor of the exchequer, Sir John Simon, addressed the Commons with the kind of optimism that hallmarked Askey's style: 'We are getting back to normality. *Band Waggon* will be back on the air next week.' Arthur boasted of the show's mention in *Hansard* until his death. The little man's humour and resilience perfectly complemented the mood of the country on the threshold of its darkest hour."[4]

It should also be noted that on October 11, 1939, Sir Samuel Hoare speaking in the House of Commons described *Band Waggon* as "perhaps the most popular programme of all time."

Unquestionably, 1938 and 1939 were the two most important years in Askey's life. He may have been around for more than a decade, but now he was hailed as something special. The theatrical publication, *The Era* (December 30, 1938) wrote that 1938 was the year of Arthur Askey, Tommy Trinder and Issy Bonn.[5] "One may not unfairly regard Arthur Askey as a broadcasting comedian who has now left his cosy flat at Broadcasting House for the outer world. One finds to one's delighted astonishment that Arthur is even better in the tour ensemble than as but a fleeting voice. His minimificent stature, of which he makes such excellent play, his cunning miming — those flying motions in his seagull song, for example — mark Askey as one in the very front rank." A critic in the *Daily Herald* (March 18, 1939) wrote, "Everybody's heard of Arthur Askey…now you're talking. He is a comedian. He's new." As an added bonus for the year, Askey was asked to stand as one of five candidates for Rector of Aberdeen University, a title which later went to fellow comedian Jimmy Edwards, but Askey decided to withdraw from consideration.

Not surprisingly, when Arthur was asked in 1964 what had been his happiest Christmas he responded,

"Xmas 1938 — definitely. After 15 years 'struggling' I had hit the jack-pot with *Band Waggon* on radio. I was playing a West End theatre — sorting out offers for films — the world was my oyster. Christmas Day itself was a real family party — my wife, daughter, mother, father & sister — just us — nobody else, except the turkey. And we were all very proud of me!! It was indeed a very Happy Christmas."[6]

Band Waggon was first heard on Sunday, January 5, 1938, and was not a success. The second show was equally forgettable despite the presence of American singer Harry Richman. Other guest stars included George Formby (episode nine) and Elizabeth Welch (episode sixteen). After the third show, John Watt decided to cancel the series once the first six episodes had aired. Happily, Askey and Murdoch (who had not been heard in the first four episodes) had other ideas, as they began to contribute more and more jokes and ideas to the show, and with Askey's contributing his own dialogue.

"We used to have conferences and put up ideas about the show, but it was sometimes a regular nightmare hunting round for the right material — just racking our brains for something we could hang our hats on, so to speak."[7]

The conferences lasted some three hours at a time. Arthur, Richard Murdoch, Gordon Crier and Vernon Harris did most of the talking, while Penny Worth took notes. Great care was taken in the preparation of the scripts, with what might seem to be ad-libbing very carefully written out. The spontaneity came from Askey's and Murdoch's time on the variety stage and their understanding of split second timing.

One continuing joke involved Arthur's "coms" or combinations, one-piece underwear consisting of both shirt and long underpants. "Coms were fairly rained on me," commented Askey. "Long coms, short coms, thick coms, thin coms, miniature coms, outsize coms, and just ordinary coms. There were so many that my wife used to pick out the serviceable ones, make them up in bundles, and send them off to the hospital."[8]

The first twelve episodes of series one aired, and a further six episodes for the series were announced, with the last program in series one airing on May 4, 1938. In fact, series two ran a full twenty-four episodes, beginning on Wednesday, October 5, 1938, and ending on March 15, 1939. The first five shows in series one ran forty-five minutes, and the remaining shows in series one and all of series two ran a full hour. For the final broadcast, the best moments from the previous shows were recreated. There was a vacancy — a permanent one — on the roof of Broadcasting House.

Band Waggon was not the only radio show on which Askey was heard in 1938. On April 21 of that year, he headlined a variety bill from the Royal Bath Hotel, Bournemouth. Sharing the airwaves with him were husband-and-wife singing team, Anne Ziegler and Webster Booth, nightclub entertainer and sophisticated female impersonator Douglas Byng, and Billy Bissett and His Canadians with the Canadian Capers. On December 11, 1938, he hosted A "Grand Radio Concert" from the Majestic Theatre, Reigate. On August 4, 1939, while *Band Waggon* was on hiatus, Askey was the guest star on the popular series, *Let's Go to Town*, hosted by Leslie Mitchell.

A writer, back in December 1938, made the very valid point that *Band Waggon* was a slapstick comedy put over only with the use of sound:

"The thing he has discovered is that it is possible, in spite of everything, to put slapstick over the microphone. A remarkable discovery. For slapstick seemed the one certain line that broadcasting should not attempt. It so obviously depends on sight, upon seeing people getting tangled up in things, and fall over things, upon the facial expression of the discomfited who fall and pick themselves up and start again with fresh confidence only to fall once more; upon in fact the whole elaborate, fantastic, traditional and entirely visual business of clowning."

Askey concurred,

"First of all, I forgot the microphone, and imagined I was entertaining people who could really see me. Then I have found that the essential thing to make folks laugh is what I might call circus comedy — a man falling over something, tumbling down a ladder or something of that sort, Mark you, it took some time to hit the right note. In a way you are groping in the dark when you can't see the response.

"But we had some interesting proofs that the response was there all right. One provincial newspaper, for example, made an inquiry as to why telephone calls were fewer between eight and nine-thirty on Wednesday night, and came to the conclusion that it was because people were listening in to *Band Waggon*."[9]

On *Band Waggon*, he did slapstick things and things happened to him. On a Christmas show, he had Richard Murdoch assisting in the making of a Christmas pudding. Orders were shouted out and it was as if the audience saw them being taken care of. With every obvious fault on Murdoch's part, Askey would respond, "I Don't Suppose It Matters." An explosion indicates all has ended in disaster, and the obvious response now from two voices is "I Don't Suppose It Matters." Here is audio comedy blended with unseen slapstick comedy and clowning. "You can do anything with the microphone," Arthur explained.[10]

The final series of *Band Waggon* ran for eleven episodes, beginning on Saturday, September 16 and ending on Saturday, December 2, 1939. They were each forty-five minutes in length. According to historian Mark McKay only a very few episodes from the entire three seasons survive: March 9, 1938 (fifteen minutes of extracts), January 18, 1939 (complete program), March 15, 1939 (extracts issued as a three-record set on HMV 78 RPM recording, BD 693, 694 and 695), and September 30, 1939 (complete program).

Aside from the above-mentioned HMV recordings, the company also released other excerpts from *Band Waggon*: "Blacking Out the Flat" (recorded November 9, 1939, BD 764), "Big and Stinker's Parlour Games" (recorded November 13, 1939, BD 784), "Big and Stinker Minding the Baby" (recorded April 14, 1940, BD 841), "The Proposal" (recorded at a concert for British troops in France, April 25, 1940, C 3173), "The Seagull Song" and "More Chestnut Corner" (recorded at the same troop concert, BD 855), "Big and Stinker's Moment Musical" and "Talking Shop" (recorded July 21, 1940, BD 870).[11]

Band Waggon on Stage

The stage rights to *Band Waggon* were acquired by band leader and impresario Jack Hylton. The show opened on December 26, 1938 at London's Princes Theatre (now the Shaftesbury Theatre) for a four-week season, and then, on July 3, 1939, it opened at the London Palladium, following a successful regional tour that included three weeks at the Birmingham Hippodrome in March. Aside from Askey, Murdoch and Syd Walker, the show also featured Tommy Trinder. A month later, Askey and Murdoch, without Trinder, began work on a screen version of *Band Waggon*.

The stage version of *Band Waggon* contained a feature titled "New Voices," and one of the very young comedians was a fourteen-year-old named Ernie Wise, who, according to Askey, wore a tuxedo and clogs, sang and tap-danced. Ernie Wise was, of course, to team with Eric Morecambe and become the legendary Morecanbe and Wise. As Wise commented at the October 1974 Variety Club's tribute to Askey on his 50th anniversary in show business, "Arthur and I are entirely different in our profession. I am half a double act, and he is half a single act." Eric Morecambe added, "Here is a man who has been entertaining us for years — whether we wanted him or not."

The London Palladium show was a tremendous hit with audiences, male members of whom were at one point invited to dance down the aisles with the chorus girls to the music of the "Beer Barrel Polka." The show was frenetic and a party spirit was pervasive. Following the London Palladium engagement, *Band Waggon* went back to touring, with Max Wall replacing Tommy Trinder.

In the summer of 1940, Askey and Murdoch revived the stage production under the new title of *Blackpool's Own Band Waggon*. It played the summer season at the Opera House in the North of England seaside resort. Joining Askey and Murdoch were Norman Evans, the Albert Sandler Trio, Sid Seymour and His Mad Hatters, Willie West and McGinty, and comedian Norman Evans. In his autobiography, Askey reports that his salary was now 350 pounds a week. Presumably that weekly salary included one week in September 1940 when Arthur was too ill to appear and George Formby, who lived only four miles away, took over.

"Only the best people come to Blackpool," Askey told his audience. When it responded with a resounding, "Yes!" the comedian asked, "Well, what are you lot doing here!"

When World War Two began in September 1939, the BBC moved its variety department from London to an empty house in the West of England city of Bristol.[12] The first wartime broadcast of *Band Waggon* was on September 16, 1939. Askey was working in the screen version and getting him down to Bristol proved difficult. Gas or Petrol rationing had started, and the comedian had enough in the tank of his car to get him to Bristol but not to return to London. John Watt came up with a solution:

"He bought an extremely old Humber for five pounds. He said he didn't know whether it had an engine but it certainly had a tank. On Saturday night the petrol tank was duly filled, and on Sunday night (after we had played *Band Waggon*) with the help of a piece of rubber tubing, it was duly emptied. The carcass was then sold to the scrap-heap for thirty shillings."[13]

As part of the war effort, Askey and Murdoch flew to France on April 12, 1940, to entertain the British troops there with selections from *Band Waggon*. The pair were joined by Jack Hilton and His Band, together with Gracie Fields, who had already been active entertaining the British troops

Askey and Murdoch broadcasting during World War Two.

in France. The group was also invited to perform at the Paris Opera House in front of the French President, and had the pleasure of meeting Maurice Chevalier, a thrilling experience for Gracie Fields. Sadly, the so-called "phony war" came swiftly to an end and threats of a German advance towards Paris led to Askey's making a quick return to the relative safety of England.

Surprisingly, it was not until late September 1939, a couple of weeks after the outbreak of World War Two, that the BBC allowed its comedians to tell jokes ridiculing Hitler. "Before they war they had to lay off for fear of causing diplomatic complications."[14] As a result, Askey told of training 5,000 parrots to fly over to "old Nasty's house at Birsdgarden" and sing, "We'll be glad when you're dead you rascal you!" On *ITMA*, Tommy Handley told of famous moustaches that had made their way in the world, "including one called Adolf."

The war did not affect Arthur personally until June 21, 1941, when he visited Birmingham's Corporation Street Employment Exchange to register for National Service. A new order under the Registration of Employment Order required men born between June 1 and December 31, 1900 to register. Happily for Arthur, he was never called up for any physical fight with the Nazis.

Band Waggon was heard on radio again, on June 8, 1940, when the touring stage version was broadcast live. There was a one-time revival, on November 13, 1947, to celebrate the BBC's Silver Jubilee. Replacing Syd Walker was Fred Yule. To celebrate the BBC's Golden Jubilee, on December 28, 1971, Askey and Murdoch revived their flat on the roof of BBC Broadcasting House, and discovered that since 1939 the corporation had been broadcasting using Askey and Murdoch's electricity. For that nostalgic revisit, the couple was joined by Wallas Eaton and Anthea Askey.

An earlier attempt at a reunion of Askey and Murdoch was *The Arthur Askey Show*, which also featured Pat Coombs and writers Bob Monkhouse and Denis Goodwin. It was first heard on September 30, 1958.

Living It Up

In 1957, and televised in two series from April 12 through May 10 and from October 27 through December 1, Askey and Murdoch moved over to commercial television for a series titled *Living it Up*, in which the couple was living in a penthouse at the top of Television House, the Association Rediffusion Building on London's Kingsway. The new series was written by Sid Colin and Talboth Rothwell (of *Carry On* fame), and co-starred Hugh Morton, Billy Percy, as the milk man, and Danny Ross, as a prop boy. Askey was paid 750 pounds per show.

After the closing credits, the comedian would re-appear and make comments to the studio audience, usually announcing it had not laughed much during the show, but was improving its reaction when it was over. Askey was certainly not happy with the critical response to *Living It Up*, which was far from enthusiastic.

"Askey has such a boisterous genius for bursting through the fabric of any TV show that anything he does is watchable," wrote Philip Purser in the *News Chronicle* (October 28, 1958). "But these two kindly, likable and talented men deserve better material." In the *Daily Mail* (October 28, 1958), Peter Black wrote, "In its 27 minutes I counted two jokes that sounded as though someone was trying. The rest were typical of a lazy show that was being flung into the public' face like a gesture of complaint."

Norman Cook in the *Liverpool Echo* (October 28, 1958) was in a more reflective mood:

"Askey is television's throw-back to the circus clown or provincial music-hall comedian at his crudest and corniest...But I cannot help hoping that the day will come when, thanks largely to television, our taste in comedy will have matured sufficiently for us to be less dependent on the capering clown and more attached to the subtle comedy actor...Askey can still be very funny. But his style of comedy has outlived its age."

Jack Hylton's production of *Living It Up* reminds one of the close relationship between him and Arthur Askey. During World War Two, Askey and his family stayed at a cottage on Hylton's estate near Oxford. The comedian writes glowingly of Hylton, whom he first met when the notion of a film version of *Band Waggon* was first mooted. "I found him a fascinating character and we struck up a friendship that lasted over twenty-five years [as of Askey's writing his autobiography]. He was a real extrovert and his motto was 'If you think champagne, you'll drink champagne'.... He had several cars, several horses, and assorted mistresses. He lived like Nero of old and was naturally a good Socialist!"[15]

Jack Hylton (1892-1965) came to fame in the early 1920s with his dance band, soon gaining the title of "Britain's King of Jazz" — and just like Paul Whiteman, the American King of Jazz, the music he performed had little to do with jazz in its purest form. (In 1932, Hylton and Whiteman made a transatlantic broadcast together.) Jack Hylton made his screen debut in 1935 with *She Shall Have Music*, which is a fun production but also demonstrates how little charisma Hylton actually has and how he is better suited to radio, better heard than seen.

He became an impresario in the early 1940s, producing stage shows (including Royal Command Performances) and later television productions under the banner of Jack Hylton Television Productions Ltd. For many years, Hylton was also financially responsible for the London Philharmonic Orchestra.

Despite the demise of *Band Waggon*, Arthur Askey's radio career was far from over. It was followed by *Big's Broadcast*, broadcast from Bangor in North Wales for eight weeks, beginning August 1, 1941. It was promoted with the announcements, "Radio's silly little man takes over for half an hour." Beginning on February 15, 1942, *Big Time* co-starred Askey with Florence Desmond and Jackie Hunter. *Forever Arthur*, with Kenneth Horne, and intended to recapture the impact of *Band Waggon* was set in a lighthouse and begin broadcasting on April 22, 1946.

Jack Hylton.

At the close of World War Two, Askey participated in *Atlantic Spotlight*, advertised as an NBC Exchange Programme, featuring the comedian, Dorothy Carless, Gene Crowley, and Lionel Gamlin in London, and Bob Hope, Jerry Colonna and Ben Grauer in New York. The show was broadcast from 5:30 through 6:00 p.m. on the General Forces Network on January 27, 1945.

Bob Monkhouse and Denis Goodwin both wrote and participated in *Hello Playmates*, which introduced two comediennes who were to become favorites on radio and television, Irene Handl and Pat Coombs. The show was first broadcast on May 31, 1954. *Askey Galore* was the radio version of the popular television series, starring Askey with magician David Nixon, Sabrina, and singer Vanessa Lee (wife of Peter Graves). It began on radio on January 30, 1957.

How Do You Do?, first heard on the BBC's Light Programme on January 20, 1949, was described as a new form of radio entertainment wherein the comedian visited various families in their homes and attended parties there. He was supported by daughter Anthea, accordionist Delmondi and Jimmy Bailey at the piano.

Beginning on June 17, 1952, Askey was heard on *Arthur's Inn* with Brian Reece (radio's character of P.C.49) as the managers of a ramshackle restaurant. Alan Melville, Bob Block and Bill Harding wrote the scripts,

A comedy pose from the 1940s.

and bringing glamor to the program were Sally Ann Howes and Diana Decker. The critics were not impressed, with the *Daily Herald* (June 18, 1952) noting the two men "made heavy going of dull material liberally laced with chestnuts." In January 1957, Askey partnered with magician David Nixon on a short-lived panel show titled *Do You Mind?* (Somehow one doubts the skills of a magician come across well on radio, but it was another time and David Nixon was then the most popular magician in the country.)

The most prominent of radio panel shows on which Askey participated was *Does the Team Think?*, a parody of the serious program, *Any Questions*, on which celebrities answered questions from a studio audience. Both the questions and answers were presented for laughs. The series was devised in 1957 by Jimmy Edwards and aired on the BBC's Light Programme (Radio Two). Askey was an occasional guest on the second series, beginning June 1958, and became a regular on series fifteen, beginning in October 1970, replacing Tommy Trinder, and now heard on Radio Four. He continued on *Does the Team Think?* through its final broadcasts in 1976.

With David Attenborough, Arthur Askey holds the record for the most appearances on the BBC's *Desert Island Discs*, on which celebrities are invited to select the recording they would most like to have with them if stranded on a desert isle. Askey's first time on the show was on April 2, 1942, and his choices included Jack Hylton and His Orchestra playing "Three Little Bears," Paul Robeson singing "Canoe Song," Gracie Fields singing "Sing As We Go," classical pieces by Mendelssohn, Schubert and Tchaikovsky, and the comedian himself on *Band Waggon*. He was back again on August 21, 1955, and classical pieces dominated, together with Johnnie Ray singing "Cry" and Danny Kaye singing "The Inchworm." For his third visit, on December 23, 1968, classical pieces were interspersed with recordings by Julie Andrews, The Beatles, Val Doonican, and Arthur himself, with Dickie Murdoch performing "The Proposal." For the final visit, on December 26. 1980, The Beatles were back, along with Jack Hylton, as well as Stanley Holloway and more classical pieces.

---

1. Angela Jeans, *The Man Who Was My Husband*, p. 85.

2. Tommy Trinder (1909-1989) was a comedian who greeted his audience with "You lucky people." He was immensely popular on stage, radio and film, but virtually unknown outside of his native Britain.

3. Quoted in "Biography: Arthur Askey."

4. John Fisher, *Funny Way to Be a Hero*, pp. 175-176.

5. Issy Bonn (1903-1977) was a Jewish comedian and actor. "Too often," wrote the critic in The Era, "I have sat out some comic business of stage Jews feeling profoundly uncomfortable because of this fact. But there is none of this with Issy Bonn, nor does he deal in those slanderous allegations of cunning, greed and treachery. He stands, smiles, and passes his jokes and malapropisms, with him we laugh with, and not at, Jewry."

6. Arthur Askey letter to Elizabeth Jay, October 21 1964, Anthony Slide Collection.

7. "Arthur Askey the Man Who Made *Band Waggon*."

8. Ibid.

9. Ibid.

10. Grace Wyndham Goldie, "Our Arthur," p. 1202.

11. As Mark McKay documents, Band Waggon has been featured on other recordings: *Fifty Years of Radio* (1972), *Memories of Band Waggon, Happidrome and Other Great Wireless Comedy Shows* (1980), *The Golden Age of Arthur Askey* (1986), and the CD *Band Waggon* (1990).

12. The BBC later took over an underground fortress that had been built as a railway tunnel and used it to house the BBC Symphony Orchestra and its conductor Adrian Boult. When air raids on Bristol increased, the music department was moved to Bedford and the variety department to Bangor in North Wales. However, in the fall of 1943, variety moved back to London.

13. Angela Jeans, *The Man Who Was My Husband*, p. 95.

14. "Okay to Kid Hitler on British Radio," p. 19.

15. Hylton had two daughters with his mistress, Frederika "Fifi" Kogler. He was married twice.

As Charley's (Big-Hearted) Aunt.

CHAPTER FOUR

On Screen

Arthur Askey's first film appearance was far from auspicious. For the princely sum of ten pounds, he was asked in 1937 to play a waiter in a seventy-five minute British Lion feature in which a group of British "stars" visit and perform at a nightclub. Among the so-called stars were singers Flotsam and Jetsam (B.C. Hilliam and Malcolm MacEachern), Elizabeth Welch, Evelyn Dall and Turner Layton, comedians David or Davy Burnaby, Billy Bennett and Ethel Revnell and Gracie West, Carroll Gibbons and the Savoy Orchestra, and, most importantly (from a historical perspective) African American entertainers the Nicholas Brothers and Buck and Bubbles.

Askey prepared various waiter jokes, but when he arrived at the studio he was told to lose his glasses, which it was pointed out waiters did not wear, approach David Burnaby's table and announce the next act, the Whirlwind Skaters, two men and a woman who perform on roller skates. (For some reason, Askey remembered the act as the Four Marvellos.) Cinema audiences never got to hear any of the jokes that Arthur had come up with, including such brilliant lines as:

"Waiter, do you serve lobsters?"

"Yes sir, sit down — we serve anybody!"

When *Calling All Stars* was released in March 1937, Askey sent his wife to see the film at London's Piccadilly Theatre. Without his trademark glasses, she failed to recognize her husband.

However, as a result of his appearance in *Calling All Stars*, Pathe Newsreel invited him to appear in one of its entertainment shorts, *Pathe Pictorial*, released in 1937. He sang "The Bee Song."

Two further *Pathe Pictorials* followed. In 1937, he performed "The Moth." And in 1938, he performed "A Pretty Bird" and "Big-Hearted Arthur."

Band Waggon

Appropriately, Arthur Askey's film career began in earnest with a screen adaptation (of sorts anyway) of his radio hit, *Band Waggon*. The opening credits in fact identify it as "Radio's Greatest Success." Richard Murdoch was an integral part of the cast, and comedy (of a sort) was also provided by Moore Marriott, who appears in most of Askey's wartime films. Long associated with Will Hay in the 1930s, Moore Marriott is most closely associated with Askey in the 1940s. Jack Hylton and his Band who had been surprisingly good in the 1935 film, *She Shall Have Music*, return to the screen for one last time in *Band Waggon*.

Band Waggon began filming at Gainsborough Pictures' Islington Studios at the beginning of May 1939. Because of blackout restrictions, production was moved to the Shepherd's Bush Studios at Lime Grove, the roof of which was utilized to represent the roof of Broadcasting House. The comedian's later wartime films were all shot at Shepherd's Bush. Askey recalled the film was directed by "an excitable Frenchman" named Marcel Varnel:

"He had directed the Crazy Gang pictures and his greatest asset was his speed. He was paid a bonus which depended on how quickly he finished a film. His big catchphrase was 'Vy are ve vaiting?' He used to sit under the camera waving his handkerchief during every shot, and when he was satisfied he always said, 'Cut — print — give me a view-finder — ooh, Christ!' That was when he banged his head on the camera as he sprang up from his chair."[1]

All of Askey's Gainsborough films were produced by Edward Black, who had started with Gainsborough as studio manager in the late 1920s.

Once production had moved to Shepherd's Bush, the shooting of the interiors of the opening scenes were filmed. (Initially, it seems *Band Waggon* was actually filmed in sequence.) R.B. Marriott of *The Era* was introduced to the Askey/Murdoch menagerie, obviously unseen but well discussed on radio:

"Perhaps the first thing that struck one forcibly was the appearance of Lewis the Goat, about whom we have heard so much but of whom we have seen so little. Lewis certainly lives up to his radio reputation. He looks a trifle awed with the filming business, but soon settled down in his pen-cum-kennel placidly chewing the geraniums that grew in profusion in small boxes outside his home.

"Henrietta the Hen and Gerald the Cock, the famous chickens, definitely showed temperament. Perched in an improvised coop high up on a chimney-pot, the two at first refused to appear before the camera."[2]

Gainsborough Pictures' resident art director Alex "Vetch" Vetchinksy (despite his name born in London) did a fine job of visualizing how the Askey/Murdoch flat might look. "It's uncanny," said Askey, "This bloke Vetchinsky seems to know our flat better than we do! The art director must know all our home secrets." Vetchinsky had only listened to *Band Waggon* once on the radio, but he had seen the stage production.[3]

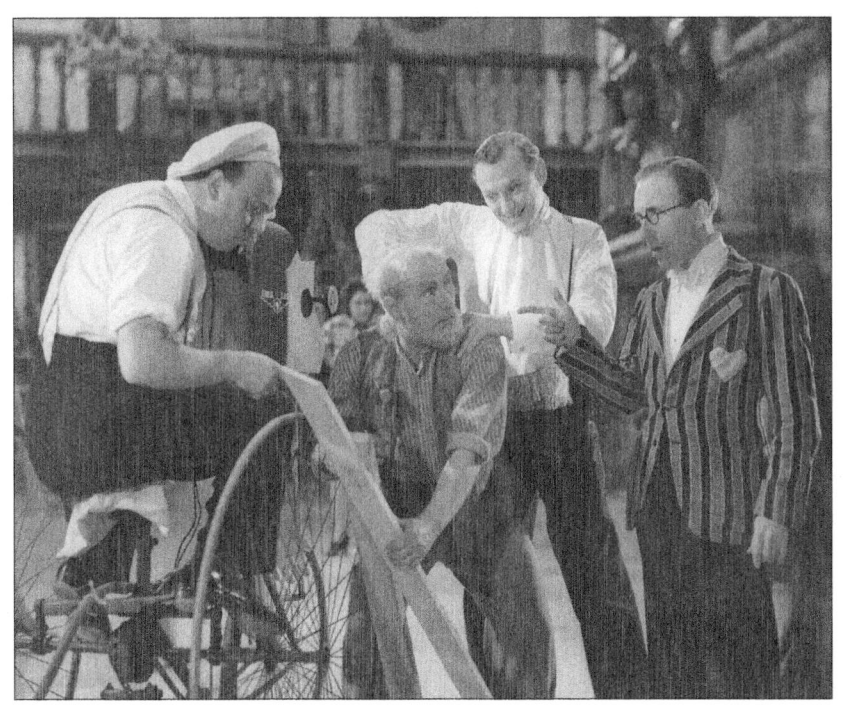

Band Waggon *with Arthur, Moore Marriott and Richard Murdoch.*

After being discovered in their flat on the roof of Broadcasting House, Askey and Murdoch are evicted by the BBC's officious and bombastic BBC executive and, apparently, talent scout John Pilkington (Peter Gawthorne) and Commissioner Wally Patch. Driving home that night, Pilkington gets a puncture from broken glass put in the road by Jack Hylton and His Band. While he waits for a repair, Pilkington is treated to a show, at the Jack-in-the-Box Roadhouse, by Hylton and singer Pat Kirkwood in the hope that they will be signed by the BBC. It is to no avail after Pilkington discovers who is responsible for his puncture. Meanwhile, Askey and Murdoch have cheaply rented a castle, with such a low rent because unknown to them it is haunted. The castle's janitor is Moore Marriott. Discovering a secret television studio in the castle, used by Nazi agents, the boys along with Hylton, his band, and Pat Kirkwood put on a show. Well, you do of course. The show is broadcast over the BBC television wave length. After calling in Scotland Yard and defusing a bomb, all ends well with Askey, Murdoch and company being given a BBC contract, and everyone singing a popular British song of the period, "Hands, Knees and Boomps-a-Daisy." It is pretty ridiculous, but not un-entertaining. There are brief cameos by some BBC personalities, commentator Michael Standing, gardening expert Mr. Middleton and announcer Jasmine Bligh. And its six featured songs are pleasing: "The Melody Maker," "The Only One Who's Difficult Is You," "After Dark," "Heaven Will Be Heavenly," "A Pretty Bird," and the aforementioned "Hands, Knees and Boomps-a-Daisy."

Writing in *The Observer*, the doyenne of British film critics, C.A. Lejeune wrote,

"This is 'Big's' first film and he is still not quite certain of his medium. He tends to mug and over-act. Accustomed to the footlights and the microphone, he hasn't realised yet how the camera amplifies every grimace and gesture. But the promise of real comedy is there. The little man has pathos. Like all great clowns, from Grock to Chaplin, he knows how to command sympathy as well as laughter. You laugh with Arthur Askey — never at him."[4]

The most telling of reviews came from the anonymous critical for the *Illusytrated London News* (February 17, 1940), who noted,

"It appears to have been assumed, in the usual foolish way, that their [Askey and Murdoch] radio reputation would of itself make a film success."

It did not.

H.M.V. Recordings

Not only was Askey busy with film and stage work, he was also under contract to H.M.V. (His Master's Voice) to make two records every month over a two-year period. His recording career began in earnest at H.M.V. in 1938/1939 with "I Pulled Myself Together and "Ding Dong Bell" (recorded December 1938), "Knitting" and "The Worm" (January 1939), and "All to Specification" and "The Cuckoo" (January 1939). Askey's war-related recordings perhaps begin with "Follow the White Line" and "FDR Jones" (recorded November 1939) He claimed to have been the first to sing the classic World War Two hit, "We're Going to Hang Out the Washing on the Siegfried Line," written in 1939 by Jimmy Kennedy and Michael Carr. But credit for that should probably go to the Two Leslies

(Leslie Sarony and Leslie Holmes). There is also a film record of African American and British-based Adelaide Hall singing the song to the troops in 1939. Askey also claims to have been first to sing another 1939 hit, "Run Rabbit Run," but that was written by Noel Gay and Ralph Butler for Flanagan and Allen.

That being acknowledged, it must also be noted that in October 1939, H.M.V. was promoting "Records to Brighten Your Black-Out," and included were two of Askey's: "Hands, Knees and Boomps-a-Daisy"/"We're Going to Hang Out the Washing on the Siegfried Line" and "Kiss Me Goodnight Sergeant Major"/"How Ashamed I Was."

Among Askey's wartime hits are "Two Little Doodle Bugs" and "C'est La Guerre" (recorded April 1940), "Fanny, Fanny" (a novelty song about a fan dancer) and "(Bomb Bomb) Get in Your Shelter" (November 1940), "When That Man Is Dead and Gone" and "Come and Have a Drink at the Victory Arms" (very prematurely recorded in March 1941), "You Mustn't Forget the Girl You Left Behind" and "Hello to the Sun" (October 1941), "What a Nice Lot of Nazis They Are" and "The Thing-Ummy Bob" (January 1942), and "Hold Your Hats On!" and "Twenty-One Shillings a Day" (July 1942).

Arthur's most controversial wartime recording was "Thanks for Dropping in Mr. Hess," released by H.M.V. in July 1941, and poking fun at Deputy Fuhrer Rudolf Hess's surprise flight to Scotland in May of that year. The War Office banned the song for fear it would damage morale among the military, although why seems hard to understand. The song was coupled with "The Stuttering Sergeant," which might more reasonably be banned as politically incorrect.

There were just as many non-war related songs, including the monologs "The Channel Swimmer" and "The Fair Rosamunde" (May 1941)," "Sarah, Sarah" and "She Was Very, Very, Very Shy" (August 1940), "All through a Glass of Champagne" and "Please Leave My Butter Alone" (January 1940), "The Budgerigar" and "The Pixie" (May 1941), "The Baa Lamb" and "The Death Watch Beetle" (October 1941), "The Bunny Rabbit" and "The Frog" (January 1942), "The Ant" and "The Flu Germ" (March 1942), "It's Spring Again" and "I Want a Banana" (April 1942), and "The Moth" and "The Villain Still Pursued Her" (recorded for ENSA in 1943). Askey's fixation with living creatures, both animal and insect was insatiable. As late as January 1949 for H.M.V., he recorded "Every Little Piggy's Got a Curly Tail" coupled with "The Christening" and in May 1957 for Decca, he recorded "The Zebra Song" and "The Seaside Band."

Charley's (Big-Hearted) Aunt

Two weeks after completion of *Band Waggon*, Arthur was told to report back to the studio and begin work on *Charley's (Big-Hearted) Aunt*. However, it transpired that Gainsborough had not taken up his option correctly, and Jack Hylton was able to negotiate a new contract for the comedian with an extra payment of 2,500 pounds per film.

Askey was not pleased with his work in *Band Waggon*. "I thought I was terrible on the screen," he wrote to film critic Seton Margrave. "*Charley's Aunt* will, I think, be better — but had I seen *Band Waggon* before I made it, it would be better still. Oh — those terrible moments when I saw myself acting!! And striving to be funny. However with a little more experience, and a good story, I will see what I can do."[5]

Charley's Aunt is perhaps the best-known of all farces involving female impersonation, more French than English in style, despite being written by an Englishman Brandon Thomas, who appeared in the original production of the play in 1892. Brandon Thomas did not play the Fancourt Babbley who disguises himself as the title character. That role went to W.S. Penley. *Charley's Aunt* has been revived countless times on stage. It was first filmed in 1925, starring Charlie Chaplin's brother, Syd and it became a musical *Where's Charley?* in 1948, with the one constant being the costume worn by Fancourt Babbley.

Released in April 1940, the Arthur Askey version of *Charley's Aunt*, retitled *Charley's (Big-Hearted) Aunt*, is a somewhat tedious affair, despite the *Monthly Film Bulletin* (April 1940) declaring "The plot is thin but the fun is fast and furious." It has been updated and revised, but the new script by Val Guest, Ralph Smart and J.O.C. Orton is short on gags and there is nothing here that is laugh provoking as Askey follows the time-honored routine of impersonating a fellow student's aunt, although this time around she is not from Brazil (where the nuts come from) but rather Birmingham (where the nuts and bolts come from). Lending major support as Askey's collaborators are Richard Murdoch, Graham Moffatt and Moore Marriott, with solid back up provided by J.H. Roberts as the Dean, Felix Aylmer as the Provost and Jeanne de Casalis as the real aunt. Of Roberts and Aylmer, Ivor Brown wrote in the *Illustrated London News* (August 17, 1940),

"Both these players, who understand style and finesse in comedy, naturally make the rest of the film seem a crude hurly-burly of dressing up and mad escapes."

Perhaps the only truly novel aspect of the plot is to have Askey actually appearing in an undergraduate production of *Charley's Aunt*, a performance which ultimately leads to all the confusion that is to follow. (There is no explanation offered as to why this production of *Charley's Aunt* needs an orchestra.)

Viewers may not find the film hilariously funny, but apparently, in at least one scene, the actors did. Arthur, as Charley's Aunt, is taking tea with the real Charley's Aunt. When he picks up a hot tea pot and burns himself, he is advised to use the small, round pot holder. "Silly me," he responds, "I thought it was a crumpet." Jeanne de Casalis and Arthur could not stop laughing each time the line was delivered, and shooting had to be abandoned until the next morning, much to the annoyance of director Walter Forde.

One unidentified critic claimed that Arthur looked like Spencer Tracy, and that like all great comics he brought a lump to the throat even while you were laughing at him. Askey told the critic that "I've always seen myself as the dumb type of comedian, like Harry Langdon or Stan Laurel.

"But *Charley's Aunt* is the first time I've ever appeared in any character other than myself — except a dame in pantomime."

Contemporary reviews were positive. *Picturegoer and Film Weekly* (August 24, 1940) found the film, "Similar in spirit, but not in detail, to the stage farce." The other British fan magazine of the period, *Picture Show*, (September 21, 1940) observed that "two doses of Arthur Askey are better than one." The trade paper, *Kine Weekly* (April 18, 1940) described the production as "riotous," while Seton Margrave in the *Daily Mail* (August 2, 1940) wrote that Askey "is not a king's jester, but he is a jester fit for a king."

The afore-mentioned review by Ivor Brown is worth quoting at some length in that the critic captures the essence of Askey at this period in his career and ponders his future:

"Whether he is going to become the great British film-clown for whom there is now such an opening remains to be seen. Mr. Askey is essentially the brisk, perky, up-and-coming, hard as steel, sly, ingenious, nimble Little Man. He amuses us by winning his tricks whereas so many of the drolls are most attractive when they are losing them. That is what makes me wonder whether Mr. Askey will ever be at the summit of drollery's tree. It is very hard totally to amuse the British without a blend of pathos in the buffoonery. Mr. George Formby, whose new picture, *Let George Do It*, will soon be everywhere on view, has that kind of mirthful melancholy. The character whom he presents appeals to our compassion and stirs the maternal instinct with his mooncalf ways and his inability to grow up and get on terms with the world. Mr. Askey has none of that frailty. He seems always to be as tough, as thin, as fit as a fiddle, very much all there, up to scratch, and ready for any of fortune's knocks. We laugh at him in a loveless way, as at some highly ingenious marionette. But this creation of his, for all the big-heartedness of his title, is not quite a human being.

"Mr. Askey would be prudent, if he intends to put the screen before the stage, to seek a story in which he can be occasionally wan and wistful instead of always so bright and brisk. He will always have his admirers in abundance, but he will find it hard to become Britain's acknowledged darling until he can raise lumps in the throat as well as tickling the ribs."

It seems unlikely that the Arthur Askey version of *Charley's Aunt* was released in the United States. And it seems equally unlikely that Gainsborough had much faith in the film's having a long life in terms of audience appeal. In February 1941, the studio, along with the Brandon Thomas Company sold the rights to 20th Century-Fox for a reported $110,000.00. A press release from 20th Century-Fox, dated July 11, 1941, gives the amount s $125,000, and claims it is for a five-year lease. The American film, starring Jack Benny and Kay Francis, was released in August 1941. Askey would sometimes claim that it was competing with his own version, but the reality is that the Jack Benny production was not released in the U.K. until after the Askey film had ended its release.

The Ghost Train

Arnold Ridley[6] is best known to modern audiences — or at least to older members of that generation — for his performance as Private Godfrey in the popular BBC television series, *Dad's Army*. He does, however, have an earlier claim to fame, as author of the comedy-thriller *The Ghost Train*, which had a long-run on its original London production in 1923. *The Ghost Train* was filmed in 1927, 1931 and in 1941 as a vehicle for Askey and Richard Murdoch. The two are part of a group of passengers stranded overnight on a rural Cornish train station, through which a "ghost train" passes on a regular basis. Ultimately, it transpires that the train is being run by Nazi Fifth Columnists and used to carry guns and other arms. A number of popular British character players make up the cast, including Kathleen Harrison, Raymond Huntley and Herbert Lom (then billed as Herbert Lomas). More than one modern commentator has pointed out that Askey's comedic pranks are as irritating to the fellow passengers as they are to most audiences. But just imagine how truly irritating it might have been had Askey's character been presented, as Arnold Ridley, wrote as one leading man, instead of being split into two here and shared by Askey and Murdoch.

Askey's director on *The Ghost Train* was Walter Forde, one of the better British filmmakers of the period, who had been responsible for the 1931 version, starring Jack Hulbert and Cicely Courtneidge. Walter was most pleased with the earlier version, but, as he told me, he was not overjoyed about his return to the subject, and described it as "very old-fashioned."[7]

However, contemporary reviewers was more enthusiastic. The trade paper *The Cinema* (March 12, 1941) wrote,

"Sparkling comedy treatment invests old stage winner with brilliant new, entertaining life, thanks to hilarious miming and nonsensical patter of Arthur Askey, abetted by stooge Stinker Murdoch. Slick direction, rollicking stellar portrayal, powerful support, excellent production qualities."

Most critics had something of a problem with Askey's comedic efforts overshadowing the basic concept that *The Ghost Train* was a thriller.

In *The Evening News* (March 2, 1941), Jympson Harmon wrote that

"He [Askey] pops from behind doors, making faces round corners, tells spooky tales about imaginary corpses, fills cups with water from engine hoses and generally refuses to be serious when everyone else has the jitters in the haunted railway station."

Basically, as the anonymous critic for the *Sunday Chronicle* (March 23, 1941), noted Askey "ruins the picture as a thriller, but makes it as a comedy."

I Thank You

Howard Young wrote the original story for *I Thank You*, which was adapted for the screen by Val Guest and Marriott Edgar,[8] and directed by Marcel Varnel. Guest and Edgar deserve credit for the film's snappy dialogue. Filming began at the Shepherd's Bush Studios on March 24, 1941. Askey's catch phrase was, as the *Motion Picture Herald* (April 19, 1941) reported, "on the lips of old and young, rich and poor." In fact, of course, the phrase was "Ay Thang Yow." That was the film's original title, but "phonetic difficulties" resulted in a change.

I Thank You opens in what became the norm for Askey's next films with a delightful musical number, attractive both in terms of the song and the visuals that accompany it. The first shot is of the comedian lying suggestively between two young ladies, apparently in bed. In reality, while wearing his pajamas, Askey is fully-clothed and, like thousands of other Londoners at that time, is spending the night, sheltering from the blitz on a tube station platform. As he gets up and prepares himself for work, he sings the joyful Noel Gay song, "Hello to the Sun." At one point, he spies what appears to be a sleeping Adolph Hitler, but turning over the newspaper beside the individual, he discovers it is *The Jewish Chronicle*.

Askey and Richard Murdoch are variety entertainers, trying to raise money to put on a show, and plot complications result in their obtaining employment as footman and cook to Lady Randall, a plot complication that also permits Askey yet again to don female attire. There are welcome character performances from Felix Aylmer, Issy Bonn, Wally Patch and Kathleen Harrison, who indulges in a rampage of ornament smashing. There are less welcome appearances by Graham Moffatt and Moore Marriott, who always seem somewhat out of control and not necessarily working for the good of film.

After a performance by (Charlie) Forsythe, (Addie) Seamon & (Eleeanor) Farrell, the variety troupe take over the tube station platform to put on a show, with Forsythe singing "Let's Get Hold of Hitler." Lady Randall, who was herself a former music hall star, arrives, and is won over after being persuaded to come up on the makeshift stage and perform. Lady Randall is played by the brilliant music hall star, Lily Morris, but, perhaps unfortunately here, she does not sing one of her signature songs, but rather, "Waiting at the Church," made famous by Vesta Victoria.

Earlier, audiences had been treated to Askey and Murdoch singing together at the piano what might well be described as their theme song:

"I'd share my last penny with you,
"I'd split my last farthing in two
"We'll go fifty-fifty on all I've got,
"Half of everything is yours."

And, as one internet commentator has written, "Just when you think it can't get more enchanting, they both tap dance."[9]

I Thank You opened in September 1941. "Nothing could be more suited to the relaxation of the wartime audience in Britain," noted the American trade paper *Motion Picture Herald* (October 11, 1941). [Askey's] "star is still in the ascendant, and this latest comedy romp, an ebullient essay in sheer slapstick clowning, female masquerade and all, is obviously cast-iron box office material for the British picture house. Its humors are probably too native to meet with quite the same result in the American equivalent." In more recent years, a reviewer in the BBC's *Radio Times* described the film as a "tepid 'upstairs-downstairs' charade."

Back-Room Boy

Shooting began on *Back-Room Boy* in November 1941 and was completed the following month. Val Guest, Marriott Edgar and J.O.C. Orton provided the ridiculous story, and direction — which can only be described as basic — was by former assistant director Herbert Mason, who was to

Back-Room Boy, *with Graham Moffat, Moore Marriott and Googie Withers.*

make only three other films. The female stars are Googie Withers and Joyce Howard (who plays Arthur's fiancée). Eleven-year-old Vera Francis contributes more to the film, in the role of Vera, and can also be seen in *King Arthur Was a Gentleman.*

Motion Picture Herald (January 10, 1942) described Askey's role in *Back-Room Boy* as "the longest and most strenuous part he has yet had on screen." It is also his worst, and *Back-Room Boy* is assuredly the weakest of his wartime comedies. Influenced by *The Ghost Train*, the film is an uneasy mix of comedy, horror and dubious thrills. The biggest problem is that there no songs and the film must rely on the trite storyline. Basically Arthur has an important job at the BBC, providing the pips to indicate the hour, and he is fixated with time, to the annoyance of his fiancée. After an inappropriate series of pips, he is assigned as meteorologist to an isolated lighthouse off the coast of Scotland, along with Vera, a child who has smuggled herself aboard the boat taking him to the island. Googie Withers and a gaggle of girls arrive on the island after their ship is torpedoed. Half-way through, the film gets even worse with the appearance of Graham Moffatt and Moore Marriott, who can always be relied upon to put a dampener on proceedings. Why they are cast and even here is questionable; certainly Askey doesn't need supporting comedy players such as these.

After many mysterious happenings, Askey and company discover that Nazis are using the island to clear a way through a British-laid minefield. They successfully lead a Nazi warship into the minefield and are rescued by the British Navy. Askey returns to the BBC, only to discover that his job has now been given to his fiancée. In conclusion, for propaganda effect, the comedian pays tribute to the back-room boys who make the mines. The back-room boys responsible for *Back-Room Boy* deserve no such praise. *Back-Room Boy* was released in April 1942.

King Arthur Was a Gentleman

For his next two films, Arthur Askey gathered around him a small stock company of actors and writers. Both *King Arthur Was a Gentleman* and *Miss London Ltd* were written by Val Guest and Marriott Edgar, with Guest directing the second and the first in the capable, if somewhat unimaginative hands, of Marcel Varnel. There were not one but two leading ladies in the shapely forms of Evelyn Dahl and Anne Shelton. Evelyn Dahl had taken Jean Harlow's sobriquet of "The Blonde Bombshell" when she came to Britain from her native United States in 1935 as a singer with Ambrose and His Orchestra; she was both Ambrose's singer and lover until she returned to the United States for good in 1946. Certainly, she deserves praise and recognition for not fleeing back home when World War Two was declared but staying in her adopted home and generously supporting the war effort. "A really dolly girl," as Askey described her.[10] Anne Shelton was more a singer than an actress, and had become popular with her performances for the military during World War Two. Her biggest hit came in 1956 with "Lay Down Your Arms (and Surrender to Mine)." She is big girl and at one point in *Miss London Ltd* she actually compares herself to Sophie Tucker. Director Val Guest writes somewhat unflattering of Anne Shelton in his autobiography, describing her as "a cheerfully tubby teenager with the voice of a young Sophie Tucker."[11]

Like Evelyn Dahl, Peter Graves (who should not be confused with the later American actor of the same name) was as much a singer as an actor and had, indeed, appeared in many of Ivor Novello's musicals, marrying his leading lady, Vanessa Lee. In 1963, he succeeded his father and became the 8th Baron Graves. Peter Graves comes across as rather a limpid actor and for whatever reason was rejected for the draft. Jack Train had come to fame on radio's *ITMA* and was at the height of his popularity during World War Two, noted for his impersonations, which are not very memorable in *King Arthur Was a Gentleman*. Portly Max Bacon was noted for his Yiddish accent and his mispronunciation of words; he had actually toured as a drummer with Ambrose and with Evelyn Dahl. The final member of the stock company is Ronald Shiner, a comedic actor with a cockney accent who appears in an endless number of British films, and in *Miss London Ltd* does not receive screen credit. He appears only briefly as a sailor accompanying Askey off to the Navy. His role in *King Arthur Was a Gentleman* is far more important, that of a sergeant teaching Arthur how to operate a light armored vehicle known as a bren gun carrier.

King Arthur Was a Gentleman begins promisingly with Evelyn Dahl, smartly turned out in an A.T.S. uniform leading a group of similarly attired women and three men in army uniform, with the singing of "You'll Love the Army." Unfortunately, it neither gets any better nor does it continue with the same aplomb as the film mixes comedy and Arthurian legend, with Askey led to believe that he has acquired King Arthur's sword, Excalibur. *Sir Arthur Was a Gentleman* concludes in what is apparently North Africa, with Askey, Train and Bacon capturing a group of Nazi soldiers. There is an obvious attempt to inject some pathos into Askey's character, but it doesn't really work. As the critic in the trade journal, *Motion Picture Herald* (January 16, 1943) commented, Askey had been

"persuaded from the brand of comedy which has made him famous into a supposedly more 'appealing' type of role, with less of the familiar screwball and a transparent tendency towards the Chaplinesque. The experiment is not always a foregone success."

Curiously, the final shot in the film is of an arm rising out of the water, grasping the sword that Askey has rejected. The arm is quite obviously that of a woman.

Along the way, the film puts a little too much emphasis on army exercises and troop movements. The teaming of Askey and Dahl as supposed sweethearts seems a little odd, but presumably Dahl's character has a thing for little men. Anne Shelton does not get enough screen time and nor is she allowed adequately to demonstrate her vocal abilities.

What *King Arthur Was a Gentleman* does have, much to its credit, is a cameo appearance by African American drummer Freddie Crump, who does not limit his skills to performing on an actual drum kit, but, rather, works with everything from eye glasses to teeth. Crump had made his film debut in a 1929 Vitaphone short with the Norman Thomas Quintette, and, apparently, moved to Europe (basing himself in Scandinavia) in 1937. Sharing drumming credit with Crump is eight-year-old Victor (Ernie) Feldman, who later worked with Glenn Miller and Woody Herman, and immigrated to the United States.

King Arthur Was a Gentleman opened at the Empire, Leicester Square, in London, on December 4, 1942. It was promoted as the country's most ambitious wartime musical, which would seem something of an exaggeration. *Motion Picture Herald* (January 16, 1943) wrote that it "should register with those provincial audiences which have been in the established habit of swelling the Askey grosses to over 100,000 pounds per film."

Miss London Ltd

Written by Val Guest and Marriott Edgar, and directed with efficiency and some style by the former, *Miss London Ltd* was released in May of 1943. The plot, if not exactly believable, is relatively simple. American Terry Arden, played by Evelyn Dahl, arrives in London, via Lisbon, to take over her half-share of an escort agency she has inherited, Miss London Ltd, which provides young ladies to accompany military personnel on leave. She discovers that the agency, run by her partner, Arthur Bowman, played by Arthur Askey, and his assistant Joe Nelson, played by Jack Train, is in a bad way financially and in need of modernization. New girls are recruited and an officer, played by Peter Graves, with whom Terry Arden has shared a taxi provides accommodation for the agency in a hotel that he conveniently owns.

The film starts very well at Waterloo Station, with Anne Shelton, as Gail Martin, the station announcer, singing "The 8:50 Choo Choo." It's a snappy beginning but sadly the film ultimately does not live up to its opening number. Even the escorts provided by Miss London Ltd do not seem to be overly attractive. In the *Daily Herald*, P.L. Mannock described them as a "poor advertisement for British beauty."

Arthur Askey's screen time is not inordinate, and there are times when the two ladies actually dominate the film. His solo performance at the piano towards the end of *Miss London Ltd* is somewhat disappointing as, quite frankly, is "The Moth," which he performs in an attempt to persuade Romeo, the waiter, that he is Arthur Askey. Romeo, played by Max Bacon, responds, "If you are Arthur Askey, I'm Max Bacon."

Peter Graves performs a number with Evelyn Dahl, in which she is described as having "Alice Fayeable looks," and he is told by Dahl that he has "David Nivenish looks."

Episodes involving Jean Kent as an encyclopedia saleswoman seem irrelevant, as does Richard Hearne's appearance late in the film as a naval commodore obsessed with dancing. Any appearance by Richard Hearne, better known as Mr. Pastry, is a ghastly experience, and here he could so easily have been cut.

For the production, a realistic reconstruction of Waterloo Station, complete with its once popular News Theatre, station concourse, and platforms was built at Islington Studios. Some 200 extras were employed for the sequences shot on that set.

Critic P.L. Mannock, writing in the *Daily Herald* (May 8, 1943) described *Miss London Ltd* as "a sprightly production," which it is, and noted "the fun being at its best in some spots of clever mimicry." Jack Train leads the way here, with impersonations of everyone from Robb Wilton to Jack Benny's African American servant, Rochester. There are moments here when he seems, perhaps deliberately, to be impersonating Richard Murdoch in his portrayal of Askey's loyal employee and cohort at *Miss London Ltd*. Undoubtedly the most spirited impersonation, by Jack Train, Arthur Askey and Evelyn Dahl, is of the Marx Brothers, with Dahl as Groucho and Arthur as Harpo. Also praiseworthy is a remarkable, and sadly too short, devastatingly wicked impersonation of Jessie Matthews by Arlene Dahl.

Elspeth Grant in the *Daily Sketch* (May 6, 1943) found *Miss London Ltd* "has much to recommend it." While *The Stage* (May 8, 1943) enthused it was "Just the kind of musical entertainment we have been waiting for."

The fan magazine *Picture Show*'s critic, Edward Wood, agreed, describing *Miss London Ltd* as "one of the brightest non-war films.... I think films which look on the bright side of life ought to be encouraged by the Government because they have acknowledged that a happy ship, be it a military unit or a war factory, contributes in a big way to efficiency. And entertainment at a cinema when Service men and women and war workers are off duty is just as helpful as concerts given to camps and workshops."

Edward Wood went even further, suggesting that films such as *Miss London Ltd* were on a par with Hollywood musicals. Disagreeing was the anonymous film critic of *Punch* (May 26, 1943), discussing bad British films and noting that "No doubt the fact that *Miss London Ltd* is a musical film seemed to the producers to exclude them from the labour of providing it with a connected and tolerably passable plot." He continued,

"There are some gleams in the film, apart from Arthur Askey. Anne Shelton sings delightfully, and Richard Hearne as a naval officer with an irrepressible frenzy for jazz deserved a better setting. But it fails as a whole, either because its producers are under the common illusion that a plot is unnecessary if a film contains a player of outstanding excellence, or because a good plot was beyond their powers."

Miss London Ltd opened at London's Dominion Theatre in May 1943, and was still playing around the country as late as 1945.

Bees in Paradise

Only one Arthur Askey film was released in 1944, and it had actually been filmed the previous year. *Bees in Paradise* is a somewhat odd, and some might claim feminist film, in which Askey, Peter Graves, Ronald Shiner, and Max Bacon are four airman whose plane crashes near a Pacific island of which women are in control. As with bees, the males are the drones, forced to commit suicide after marriage and procreation with a female. This is Paradise Island, with, as a sign proclaims, "A New Government of the Women by the Women for the Women." As might be expected, the unbelievable plot has Askey as the love interest to more than one female.

Typically, the film opens with a song, "Keep a Sunbeam in Your Pocket." If nothing else, *Bees in Paradise* boasts a large number of songs. Val Guest deserves much praise for the use of songs which help move the plots along in all of the films that he wrote and directed. It may well that his also contributing the lyrics has something to do with this. It also has Askey again in drag, this time with a peek-a-boo Veronica Lake-style bang. The film also introduces Anne Shelton's sister, Jose Shelton, who doesn't receive screen credit. Another actress, Joy Shelton, also in film, and with credit, is no relation to either Anne or Jose.

Bees in Paradise provides Jean Kent with her first role as a leading lady. She had become a starlet with Gainsborough Pictures in 1942, making her debut in *It's That Man Again*. In Askey's *Miss London Ltd*, she had what was described as a "build-up" role, and presumably Arthur and the studio heads were pleased enough with her performance to raise her to leading lady status. Jean Kent was to go on to become a major star of Gainsborough melodramas of the 1940s, the "bad girl" of British films.

Bees in Paradise *provides Arthur with another opportunity to don female attire.*

Ronald Shiner and Max Bacon also put on dresses.

Despite attire designed to appeal to male audience members and a visit to a massage parlor, the actresses and singers in the cast pale to insignificance beside the uncredited Koringa, who, on camera, actually hypnotizes two crocodiles, This is Koringa's only known screen appearance, although she was a popular circus performer, billed as the "Only Female Fakir in the World," and with an act including her walking on the heads of five

Bees in Paradise *with Arthur and Ronald Shiner.*

crocodiles while wearing s necklace of live snakes. Despite her publicity, Koringa was not born in India, but rather France and her real name was Renée Bernard.

In an effort to replicate a tropical island, the cast and crew moved in June 1943 to the South Coast seaside resort of Torquay, staying at the Torbay Hotel, and filming on the beach and the cliffs of St. Marychurch. The visit to the so-called English Riviera was supposed to be a welcome escape from the nightly air raids in London, but on the first day of shooting some fifteen German bombers hit Torquay, with half aiming for the film location, clearly visible from the air. "I'm sorry to say, the film that was made was not worth risking one's life for," grimly wrote Askey in his autobiography.

Bees in Paradise opened at London's New Gallery Cinema on February 27, 1944. It was not well received, with the critic for *The Sketch* (March 8,

1944) noting, "It's the sort of thing that might well make a radio comedian wonder why he ever left the nice, safe, avuncular atmosphere of the B.B.C. studios." In the *Sunday Mirror* (February 27, 1944), Norah Alexander described the film as "my idea of hell," giving it three points out of ten. From a female view point, she described *Bees in Paradise* as "offensive," adding, "It's unfunny and, on top of that, it's badly made."

With completion of *Bees in Parade* Arthur had finished the eight films which he was contracted to make for Gainsborough Pictures. They were of variable quality and certainly not representative in any way of the best of British cinema during World War Two. Arthur himself pointed out that "Had they been done in normal times they would have been better."[12] It is telling that beyond *Band Waggon*, Askey devotes very little space to them in his autobiography. Certainly, the films did nothing to harm the comedian's popularity. For example, when Gainsborough staged a party in May 1942 to celebrate the filming of sixteen feature films during the blitz, it included a short, staged play, *Studio Hotel*, broadcast by the BBC, and starring was Askey, supported by Richard Murdoch, Moore Marriott, Graham Moffatt, and Phyllis Calvert. That same year — in January — *Motion Picture Herald* published a list of Britain's top ten film stars. At the bottom of the list were Charles Laughton and Leslie Howard. At the top were George Formby and Arthur Lucan ("Old Mother Riley"). In third place was Arthur Askey. The trade paper commented,

"There is not much better palliative than the comedy of Big Hearted Arthur Askey, one of the greatest drolls on stage, radio and screen, who in his second year in films has leaped to third place in the popularity poll. Askey made a name initially over the B.B.C. network, has consolidated it on the vaudeville stage and the screen. His comedy, which is reminiscent both of the conger eel and the machine guns of a spitfire, is inimitable, and he is one comedian who suffers no plagiarism."[13]

The Nose Has It

Aside from his feature films, Askey also made one informational short for Gainsborough under orders from the Ministry of Health. Marking the directorial debut of Val Guest, who also scripted, *The Nose Has It* was an eight-minute short, described by the *Documentary News Letter* (November-December 1942) as "an exceedingly funny lecture on sneezing." Val Guest, who barely acknowledges the existence of Arthur Askey in his autobiography, recalls that the short was linked to the slogan, "Coughs and Sneezes Spread Diseases." The Minister of Health was scheduled to present a lecture on the subject, but both he and his assistant had the flu, and so the assistant's assistant, Askey, presented the illustrated lecture, demonstrating "the danger of nasal germ warfare on Britain's war effort."[14]

A song survives from this period, written by Askey and Robert Rutherford, and titled "The Flu Germ." The first verse reads,

Oh I ain't no bird and I ain't no bee,
I ain't no wasp and I ain't no flee,
Who the devil am I — wait and see –
I'm a little fly germ — can't catch me!

Six verses follow along similar lines.

Going to the Dentist

In 1947, Askey appeared in three two-minute films on the subject of *Going to the Dentist* and covering "The Appointment," "The Journey" and "The Waiting Room." Sponsored by Gibbs SR toothpaste (Lever Brothers), the three films conclude with Arthur's discovering that the toothpaste has prevented his needing dental treatment.

Photographed by Shaw Wildman, they were written and directed by Richard Massingham, who produced comedy shorts on the mundane reality and general misery of British life. Back in 1933, at the start of his career, Massingham had made a traumatic comedy on the subject of a visit to the dentist titled *Tell Me If It Hurts*.

After the positive deluge of films during World War Two, Askey was to appear in only five other features, of which only one has anything to recommend it.

The Love Match

Following the success on stage and tour of *The Love Match*, a film version, filmed while the play was still entertaining audiences, released in February 1955 and shot at Beaconsfield Studios, was not an unrealistic proposition. Geoffrey Orme does a good job of adapting the play for the big screen, with Glenn Melvyn providing some additional comedy material (which may very well have been from the original play). Melvyn repeated his role of Wally Binns, and joining him from the play were, of course, Arthur Askey as his pal Bill Brown, Thora Hird as Bill's wife, Sal, and Danny Ross as Alf Hall. Shirley Eaton is more than adequate as the

Filming The Love Match.

The Love Match, *with Arthur and Glenn Melvyn.*

Brown's daughter, Rose, while William Franklyn just about survives playing the role of lodger and referee Arthur Ford.

Most delightful of all is that the film version of *The Love Match* marks a return to the screen of Robb Wilton as Mr. Muddlecombe, the magistrate, pretty much recreating his performance from the variety stage and looking not much older. He was to die two years later.

The plot of *The Love Match* on film is little different to the original play. Askey is a train driver, with Melvyn as his assistant. They are both fanatical football supporters, and at the film's conclusion drive an engine at full speed to reach Manchester in time for the match between City and United. (Nowhere is it actually stated that the two football teams in question are Manchester City and Manchester United, but one must assume this is so.) The two men are supporters of City, but Askey's son, Percy (played by James Kenney) has just been signed to a trial by United. Daughter Rose has taken up with dopey Alf, whose father is a financial supporter of United. To further aggravate Askey's character, his wife has taken in a lodger who, as a referee, had ruled against City in a crucial game.

Much of what places *The Love Match* apart from the play and from other comedies of the period is the use of locations and the natural playing of the actors. Thora Hird, for example, is a typical Northern housewife, keeping the home together while dealing with a husband who is more interested in football than his family. Danny Ross is a "gormless" idiot, with uncoordinated limbs, who represents a type of Northern comic exemplified by George Formby or James Casey as Jimmy James' sidekick Eli. Like Glenn Melvyn, Eli stuttered, and this vocal impediment was very much a part of the act — so far removed from today's obsession with political correctness. Danny Ross, who also appeared on television as Jimmy Clitheroe's stooge, usually played a character named Alf Hall.

The opening credits for *The Love Match* acknowledge the cooperation of British Railways, and three football teams, Bolton Wanderers, Charlton Athletic and Cardiff City. (Surprisingly not Manchester City or Manchester United.) Exterior scenes play a prominent role in the film, and it provides a fascinating look at commercial rail services back in the 1950s. Most of the railway scenes were filmed in Bolton. Holding the film together and carefully knitting together exterior and interior scenes is director David Paltenchi, a forgotten and obviously competent director. His real name was David Paltenghi, under which he worked as a ballet dancer and choreographer. As David Paltenchi, he made only three feature films, *The Love Match*, *Orders Are Orders* (1954) and *Keep It Clean* (1956).

The Love Match is in many ways an unusual early example of British realism on screen, more closely associated a decade later with *Room at the Top* (1959) and *Saturday Night and Sunday Morning* (1960). This is never more apparent than in the dance hall sequences shot, both exterior and interior scenes, at an unidentified Mecca Dancing Locarno Ballroom. Credit for this, of course, belongs to Paltenchi, but also to producer John Baxter, whose entire career as a filmmaker shows an interest in social realism, albeit sometimes a patronizing one. Jack Hylton, who had produced the stage production, gets major screen credit for the film ("Jack Hylton Presents"), but that credit in all probability really belongs to John Baxter.

Ramsbottom Rides Again

It was John Baxter who was to produce and direct Askey's next feature film in the fall of 1955, with Jack Hylton presenting, also for Beaconsfield Studios, with a cast also including Glenn Melvyn and Danny Ross. Betty Marsden is a poor replacement for Thora Hird as Askey's wife and Shani Wallis is an equally poor replacement for Askey's daughter. In fact everything about *Ramsbottom Rides Again* is poor from the dreadful acting through the dreadful dialogue to the direction, which is clichéd and riddled with stereotypical set-ups and camera movements. The opening titles credit Askey and Melvyn with additional comedy scenes, but they are not apparent to the viewer.

As the title suggests, it is a Western produced some ten years in advance of *Carry On Cowboy*, but in much the same vein, with Sid James, also a cowboy in the latter film, totally ill-at-ease as a cowboy with a thin line of a moustache and a very phony Americanized accent. (It is not exactly American as much of the film is set in the Canadian West.) Askey, as Bill Ramsbottom, runs a Pontefract, Yorkshire, pub, which is not doing well. When he learns that his grandfather has left him a saloon and land in the town of Lonesome, emigration is the order of business. Along with Askey, go his wife, daughter, friend Glenn Melvyn, and his daughter's boyfriend, Danny Ross. Before arriving in Canada, some thirty minutes into the film, the viewer has been treated to Askey and Melvyn as stowaways and some negative commentary on the influence of television on communal life.

In Lonesome, Askey and company must fight off Sid James (as Black Jake) and his gang of villains, but in the end they triumph, capturing Black Jake and discovering uranium on their property. There is quite a bit of stock footage, including some of African lions and a tiger, which Askey miraculously encounters in Canada. The funniest encounter is with a group of Indians, led by Sid Field's stooge, Jerry Desmonde, who is actually surprisingly realistic as Blue Eagle, the Hollywood concept of a screen Indian. His dialogue of "White Man Welcome, White Man Sit" becomes more businesslike as he discusses setting up a theatrical agency in London to provide Indians for stage, television and film work there. There is also undoubtedly the best, if not the only joke, in the film as Jerry Desmonde

Ramsbottom Rides Again.

explains that his tribe is familiar with British films and introduces a Native American Brave banging a gong in the manner of the introduction to the films of J. Arthur Rank.

In one extraordinary scene, a squaw is shown carrying on her back a papoose, who resembles Askey, and with a very obvious Indian symbol, a backward Swastika, on her clothing. It is the baby not the Swastika that disturbs our Arthur. Modern viewers will also be disturbed at Askey's parodying Glenn Melvyn's stammer and ridiculing the mentally ill.

Mention should also be made of pop singer Frankie Vaughan, who was to reteam with Shani Wallis in a 1985 London production of *42nd Street*. He shows little promise here. And then, of course, for her multitude of fans there is Sabrina, billed at the end of the list of players as an added attraction. Demonstrating her versatility she plays two unrelated roles, a ship's passenger and an Indian squaw. The second part requires no dialogue. For the first, she has three lines: "Get out, get out," "Soup" and "And you were saying."

Released in July 1956, the deluded film critic in the *News of the World* (July 29, 1956) hailed *Ramsbottom Rides Again* "as North Country as black-puddings and trotters, and much more hilarious. Big-Hearted's myriads of admirers will revel in every minute." The trade papers were equally enthusiastic, with *Today's Cinema* (May 8, 1956) describing the film as "a rich, ripe farce of a very British type." *Kine Weekly* (May 10, 1956) praised the "convincing Western atmosphere."

In its July 28, 1956 issue, the fan magazine *Picturegoer* wrote of *Ramsbottom Rides Again* that, "It is corny; it's rowdy; it's erratic; it's over-boisterous and under-directed." It is also truly awful.

Make Mine a Million

Askey and Sid James teamed up again for the former's next film, *Make Mine a Million*, released in March 1959 and opening at London's Rialto Theatre. John Baxter produced, but the direction was left to his former assistant, Lance Comfort. Jack Hylton again took overall credit for the presentation. Askey, now associated with commercial television, makes fun of his former employer, the BBC, playing a make-up man at National Television (a thinly veiled BBC) who helps buddy Sid James promote a new detergent, Bonko. Utilizing a pirate broadcasting ban, the pair insert advertisements into television programs at outside broadcasts from Ascot and the Edinburgh Festival. The van is stolen by a gang looking for gold bullion, and, needless to report, Askey captures them and become a national hero.

A number of personalities make guest appearance, among whom are Evelyn Laye, Dickie Henderson, singer Denis Lotis, Tommy Trinder, daughter Anthea, Sabrina, and racing commentator Raymond Glendenning. There is a link to the "Carry On" films here in that the writer for the former, Talbot Rothwell, wrote additional comedy scenes for *Make Mine a Million*, and the film's cast includes not only "Carry On" regular

Make Mine a Million, *with Arthur and Sid James.*

Sid James, but also Kenneth Connor in a relatively important role and an uncredited Barbara Windsor.

Make Mine a Million is the only Arthur Askey film that *Variety* felt worthy of review — on March 4, 1959. The reviewer noted that Askey's film appearances have been conspicuously less successful" than his work in other media. He continued that *Make Mine a Million* should appeal to "unsophisticated audiences," concluding,

"This neat idea should have been treated satirically and, occasionally, satire does creep into the script. But mainly it goes all out for straightforward comedy effect. A good cast brings a cheerful, boisterous good humor to its job."

Make Mine a Million marked the end of John Baxter's career in film as following its completion he became executive controller of the commercial television station, TWW (Television Wales and the West), thanks in no small part to Jack Hylton.

Friends and Neighbours

1959 might be considered a high spot in Askey's screen career with two films in release, but also it might be viewed as the end of the comedian's legitimate film career. It was in November of that year that the second Arthur Askey vehicle was released. Directed by Gordon Parry, like Askey a liverpudlian, *Friends and Neighbours* is set at the height of the Cold War and concerns an English working-class couple, Askey and Megs Jenkins, as Albert and Lily Grimshaw, who win a lottery that results in their entertaining two visitors from Soviet Russia (played by Austrian Peter Illing and Argentinian Tilda Thamar). The film involves the Russians being introduced to the complexities of British life, including the eccentricities of its licensing laws in regard to the opening hours of pubs and the game of cricket. Based on a play, presumably unproduced, by Austin Steele, a prominent television comedy writer, the film is scripted by Talbot Rothwell, some four years before he became a fixture as writer on the "Carry On" films.

Others in the cast include Danny Ross, pop singer Jess Conrad and June Whitfield, Their presence did little to enhance the film's appeal, and it was released as the second half of a double bill headed by *The Treasure of San Teresa*.

In his autobiography, published in 1975, Arthur Askey makes scant reference to his film career. Very obviously it was not important to him, despite its bringing him potentially to a far wider audience. Of the last three films he wrote,

"[*The Love Match*], made on a small budget naturally, showed a huge profit, doing marvelous business everywhere. I was on salary so I didn't make out as well as Hylton and his associates. However, it got me back into pictures and I followed it up by making *Ramsbottom Ride Again*, in which I had a small percentage interest. Then another film came up, based on my own idea of a make-up man at the BBC being bribed to put out commercials during the BBC programmes. The country was fascinated by the commercials shown on ITV at this time, so it was quite a novelty. I insisted I had an interest in this picture and put money into the production. It was the only film I ever made which lost money!....I was never made to be a Sam Goldwyn!"[15]

Rosie Dixon — Night Nurse

Arthur Askey's last film, *Rosie Dixon — Night Nurse*, is best described as a tragedy. Tragic for the comedian that he should be reduced to performing in a sex exploitation film. And tragic that here is a film aimed at the adult market, with an X-rating, but with very little sex and nudity. A disappointment on every level.

Released in January 1975, *Rosie Dixon — Night Nurse* was produced by a major Hollywood studio, Columbia. It is directed and co-written by Booker Prize-shortlisted novelist Justin Cartwright. It is his only film as director, and presumably it had made some impact on him in that his 2002 novel, *White Lightning*, concerns a washed-up filmmaker who had been responsible for a sex exploitation film titled *Suzy Crispin — Night Nurse*.

The film was executive produced by Greg Smith, who was also responsible for a series of "Confessions" films, all light-weight sex-exploitation efforts, starring Robin Askwith and all featuring well-known character players in supporting roles.

The storyline involves the efforts of Rosie Dixon (played by Debbie Ash) to become a nurse, an occupation she favors largely because of the number of good-looking doctors on staff at the hospital. The term "good-looking" is used very loosely here to describe the actors portraying such members of the medical profession. Principal billing goes to various British comedy performers, headed by the brilliant (but not here) Beryl Reid, and with Askey third billed after her and John Le Mesurier, who, as so often with this brilliant actor, seems to be ignoring the production into which he has stumbled.

Arthur plays Mr. Sunshine, whose sole contribution to the film is to whiz around in a motorized wheelchair, looking demonic and pinching the bottoms of any females that he passes. "Feeling yourself today," asks one of the doctors. "Only as a last resort," responds Arthur. In all, the comedian appears in only three scenes.

What a tragic end to a film career. And yet, in retrospect, Askey's work on screen is sadly uninspired, with only *Arthur's (Big-Hearted) Aunt* and *Miss London Ltd* worthy of attention today, and then only moderately. What is perhaps most tragic is that those judging Arthur Askey' talent from a modern perspective will do so on the basis of his films, readily available on YouTube, and they will not only be disappointed but also influenced by many of the negative comments thereon.

1. Arthur Askey, *Before Your Very Eyes*, p. 110.
2. *The Era*, August 31, 1939, p. 7.
3. Ibid.
4. Quoted in Arthur Askey, *Before Your Very Eyes*, p. 118.

5. Arthur Askey letter to Seton Margrave, February 2, 1940, Anthony Slide Collection.

6. Arnold Ridley (1896-1984) was an actor who wrote more than thirty plays. He was awarded an OBE in 1982 for services to the theatre.

7. Walter Forde interview with Anthony Slide, October 1, 1976.

8. Marriott Edgar (1880-1951) is an interesting character and one deserving of further research. Aside from his work as a scriptwriter, he wrote many of Stanley Holloway's monologues, including most famously "The Lion and Albert." He was the half-brother of Edgar Wallace.

9. "Arthur Askey: He Showed Symptoms of Being Able to Amuse," *Movietone News*.

10. Arthur Askey, *Before Your Very Eyes*, p. 128.

11. Val Guest, *So You Want to Be in Pictures*, p. 72.

12. Horace Richards, "I Thang Yow!"

13. Aubrey Flanagan, "British Stars Who Beat the Bombers," p. 35.

14. Val Guest, *So You Want to Be in Pictures*, p. 69.

15. Arthur Askey, *Before Your Very Eyes*, p. 167.

An ever-happy Arthur in the 1950s.

CHAPTER FIVE

On Stage

Arthur Askey made his West End stage debut in Rica Bromley-Taylor's *The Boy Who Lost His Temper*, which opened at the Cambridge Theatre on December 22, 1936, and ran for twenty-two matinee performances, closing on January 16, 1937. A fantasy for children, the play concerned a nine-year-old boy Keith (played by Robin Maule) whose strongest characteristic is his temper. Said temper is stolen by the imps from Temperland, and Keith becomes a little prig who is impossible to live with. The family, led by the father (played by Ian Reeves) sets out to recover the temper, which proves to be not so bad when restored to the boy.

Three roles were played by Askey and he received a favorable review in *The Times*:

"Arthur Askey is a joyous representative of Miss Tripaway, the dancing mistress, Mr. Teachem, the headmaster, and the proprietor of Selford's Emporium. There is a breeziness about all his work and an air of spontaneity in his humour that commend themselves wholeheartedly to audiences, and he brings the intimate touch of concert party to his impersonations, and scores with everything that he does."

Music for *The Boy Who Lost His Temper* was composed by Geoffrey Henman, and Askey contributed the lyrics for one of the songs:

I am Amelia Tripaway,
I teach dancing every day
Though how I make my classes pay
Is really most surprising.
I've put up with the noise
Of wayward girls and boys
But I still maintain my poise
And stop my temper rising,
And so throughout the day
You'll always hear me say —

Come on children, point your toe,
Not too fast, and not too slow.
Let your hands go to and fro,
One two three away we go.
If you make the least mistake
I'll see you through my glasses.
Though I may be slightly faded
I get through my work unaided,
There's no fear of being raided
At Tripaway's Dancing Classes. [1]

The lyrics are a far cry from the nonsense songs with which Askey was already associated.

One wonders how many watching Askey as Miss Tripaway would agree with the words of the Mayor of the Northern England city of Burnley, as reported in the *Burnley Express* (March 8, 1944), "When they had all their teachers like Arthur Askey they would be doing the right thing for education."

For his work in *The Boy Who Lost His Temper*, the comedian was paid thirty-five pounds a week. He was also rehired to repeat his three impersonations in next season's production of *The Boy Who Lost His Temper*, which ran for eighteen matinee performances at the Garrick Theatre from December 27, 1937 through January 15, 1938. Ian Reeves and Robin Maule also reprised their roles. The play was also revised for the 1938-1939 season, but with all the principals replaced, and Alexander Cameron in the Arthur Askey role.

By the summer of 1938, Askey had already been heard in *Band Waggon*, and consolidated his appeal as, arguably, the country's best-known and certainly best-loved comedian. His success did not in any way divert him from the usual summer work in concert party. This time, he was the star of *Fol-de-Rols*, with two initial weeks in Hastings and a summer season of eighteen weeks at the White Rock Pavilion in Torquay. Richard Murdoch joined Askey as co-star, and, in turn, the couple was joined by a third comedian, Jack Warner, best remembered today for his leading role in the BBC police drama, *Dixon of Dock Green* (1955-1976).

From Torquay, Askey returned to London, topping the bill with American actress/singer Molly Picon at the Shepherds Bush Empire, the Hackney Empire and the Finsbury Park Empire.

During the War, Askey gave frequent performances as the star of ENSA concerts, produced by a quasi-government agency for the troops.

Unlike many of his contemporaries, his appearances were limited to the British Isles, often at air force bases. As he noted, audiences were somewhat unreliable in that the airmen might suddenly leave in the middle of the show when the alert went off.

The Love Racket

Askey's most prominent stage appearance during the War was as the star of the musical comedy, *The Love Racket*, written by Stanley Lupino (book) and Noel Gay (music). (Gay is, of course, best known for *Me and My Girl* and its hit song, "The Lambeth Walk.") With Lupino Lane directing, and co-starring Roy Royston and Carol Raye, the show opened in Manchester on September 9, 1943, and after two weeks then moved on to Liverpool and Oxford, before opening in London at the Victoria Palace (the home of the Crazy Gang) on October 26, 1943. *The Love Racket*, advertised as "The Gayest, Happiest Musical in Town," marked Askey's musical comedy debut, as a film director no less, and it proved him to be totally at home in that medium.

The show had a film-related storyline, and even included two scenes outside Grauman's Chinese Theatre in Hollywood. One of the characters proclaimed "Baldderdash, Piffle and Poppycock." And these three words basically summed up the plot involving three married couples.

In his autobiography, Askey recalls a problem with a brief scene in which he impersonated George Bernard Shaw, wearing a Norfolk jacket, knickerbockers and a Shavian beard. The playwright's permission was required, and he said No. Eventually, Askey decided to visit Shaw in person. Again, the impersonation was rejected, but Shaw noted, "there's not the slightest reason why you shouldn't do it, because I won't be coming to see it!"

A major faux pas on Askey's part occurred on opening night when, at the start of the second act, he spied an elderly gentleman limping down the aisle with the aid of stick. He stopped the dialogue, explained what had happened so far and enquired if the gentleman was "quite comfy." The "gentleman" was the notoriously difficult critic James Agate. In his review the next day in the *Sunday Times*, he wrote of the inventiveness of great comics, such as Chaplin, George Robey and Dan Leno, and continued,

"Does one feel this about Mr. Arthur Askey? Before saying that I personally do not, let me concede that the fact that a match does not strike on my box may be as much the fault of the box as of the match. The impersonation I get from Mr. Askey's acting is that it is synthetic, in the sense that somebody invents a joke to which he then gives shape by pretending to walk like a chimpanzee or putting on a funny hat. I am prepared for the objection that half of, perhaps three-quarters, of this comedian's humour is self-invented; I must still maintain that as a comedian he fails to convey the creative sense. Is this perhaps Mr. Askey, who never stops calling attention to his lack of inches, insists a little too much on the homunculosity of the homunculus? On the stage it seems to me that this comedian's humour is physical and accidental rather than of the mind and integral. I feel I have not got at the whole truth about a performer whom half the world regards as a great clown, one who, on the radio, discards the visual appeal and is, I am told, very funny. I hasten to add that on Tuesday night an immense audience found him funnier still."

Agate's comments are certainly interesting and worthy of consideration. Askey, after all, might be described as a homunculus, a word no longer making its way into modern dictionaries but meaning a small person. His humor is to a certain, but not total, extent based on his lack of inches. Certainly, there can be few who would argue that there was an intellectual quality to Askey's humor. He is full of quips, but most of them are obvious rather than original.

In later years, Askey became friendly with Agate, meeting him at the Savage Club. "He wasn't a bad old stick really."[2]

Far more enthusiastic than James Agate was the anonymous critic for the humor magazine *Punch* (November 3, 1943), who wrote,

"Bouncing, restless, all but irresistible, Mr. Arthur Askey is the *sine qua non* of *The Love Racket*…What is his secret? He does not sing much or dance at all, but then a good comedian need not necessarily do either, even in a musical comedy. He chirps, he chortles, he banters, and he beams. Perhaps it is in the last of these accomplishments that we come closest to his secrets. Just as Alice's Cheshire Cat could reduce itself to a grin, so Mr. Askey seems at times to reduce himself to a beam — a beam through tortoise-shell glasses. It is an expression which radiates bonhomie and self-confidence. It is the kind of bonhomie which some few of us may protestingly dislike — saying that this universal ASKEY 'rubs us the wrong way' or 'does not strike on our matchbox.' It is admittedly the bonhomie of the 'life and soul' of the suburban party, the little man who produces a false beard from his waistcoat pocket, imitates a penguin or a chimpanzee at will, and evokes screams of laughter from young ladies who, between screams, declare him to be a 'caution.' But if one finds this kind of fooling tolerable at all one has to admit that it is mercurially and ubiquitously well done by Mr. Askey. His self-enjoyment is so intense that it directly communicates itself to by far the greatest part of the audience."

Of the show itself, *Punch* was less enthusiastic, finding the plot "both conventional and muddled," and the song lyrics "exceptionally unremarkable."

The Love Racket closed at the Victoria Palace on April 1, 1944, and then transferred to the Princes Theatre, opening on April 8. It closed there on July 1, 1944, after 324 performances. A nationwide tour followed, and *The Love Racket* returned to the West End, and the Adelphi Theatre, on December 23, 1944, running for thirteen performances only, until January 13, 1945.

Despite its success, Askey was later to dismiss the show as "A load of rubbish, but *very* funny. Perfect for wartime."[3]

Follow the Girls

Following *The Love Racket*, Askey decided, literally to *Follow the Girls*, an American musical that Jack Hylton had found and thought suitable for the comedian. The American production, which opened on April 4, 1944, almost simultaneously with the closure of *The Love Racket*, starred Jackie Gleason and Gertrude Niesen. The book was co-authored by Guy Bolton, often associated with P.G. Wodehouse, and various individuals were responsible for the music and lyrics.

Askey obviously bears no physical resemblance to Jackie Gleason, and the humor is decidedly different, but Hylton, Askey and audiences found him to be perfect casting. Playing opposite Askey, as a night club singer, was Evelyn Dall, an American-born entertainer who, as already noted, had come to the United Kingdom in 1935 and became known as the "Original Blonde Bombshell."

Rehearsals began in August 1945, *Follow the Girls* opened in Manchester and had a brief tour before coming to London and His Majesty's Theatre on October 25 of that year. Producing and directing was Walter Forde, a pre-eminent British film director of the 1930s and 1940s who had commenced his career as a music hall comedian and fully understood comedy.

Follow the Girls ran for 575 performances, and closed on February 22, 1947.

Pantomime

There were certain constants in Arthur's life, and one was the annual Christmas-time appearance in pantomime. Pantomime or "Panto" had always played a big part in Askey's early life — as a child, his family took him to the theatre once a year, and it was to see a pantomime. As regular as Christmas comes around in the United Kingdom, so does pantomime, that glorious seasonal entertainment in which the principal boy is always played by a female star with good legs and the dame is always played by a leading comedian renowned for how grotesque he might appear in feminine attire. Often, the "ugly sisters" are played by two male comedians. There are, of course, exceptions, and in recent years the exceptions seem to have become the norm. Askey was there at the changeover, when male pop stars such as David Whitfield and Engelbert Humperdinck proved themselves capable principal boys in the title role of *Robinson Crusoe*.

Quite rightly and astutely, one critic in the 1970s wrote,

"The real national theatre is not on the South Bank at all, it's in the provinces, at pantomime time."[4]

Askey would probably have agreed with the critic. He was no fan of a national theatre, pointing out, "If a man is good at his job he'll make a living without the help of a National Theatre."[5]

In typical conservative fashion, he raged,

"I do not believe in these sponsored efforts. The object of the theatre is first and foremost to entertain and amuse the people and, therefore, it should be run on a commercial basis. Give the public the plays, musical comedies, farces or reviews it wants. Don't let some hoary-bearded civil servant decide to put on a Greek tragedy that a very small minority would want to see, and for which you would have the privilege of paying for in your taxes."[6]

In 1982, Askey explained — sounding a little irritated — what a pantomime dame should be,

"The dame is really the pivot of the pantomime in that the dame must always be played by the principal comedian, as the principal boy should be played by a woman. Those are the two basics of a pantomime. Now a real dame must be a butch man. In other words, under his skirt, you ought to be able to see his trousers, and know he's a man, He's Charley's Aunt….In recent years we've had that little touch of effeminacy coming in, you know, where the fellow you're not quite sure if he's a man or a woman. The dame should definitely be a man. And the audience should know he's a man. And the kids in the audience should now he's a man. I go in the dressing room, I don't put any different make-up on to the ordinary pancake slap, and no eyebrows or anything. I go on as Arthur Askey, with a hired wig and a hired frock…and play me…. No falsetto voice or anything like that."

Writing in *The Stage* in 1954, Barry Cryer described Askey as "a wonderful role model. No matter what he pretended, every child knew it was a silly little man dressed up."[7] Put simply, as Askey explained, "When a producer books me that's all he wants. And that's all he gets."[8]

The role of the dame was, of course, not only a starring one, but a part that would often find the character on stage alone with the audience. Askey understood, as one critic noted, that "a solo turn can really bring the house down."[9]

Babes in the Wood was a favorite Askey pantomime, with his usually playing the nurse "Big Hearted" Martha. However, for the 1934/1935 season of *Babes in the Wood* at the Theatre Royal, Nottingham, he was cast as Cheeky Sammy. The role of the Dame was taken by Charles Harrison. It was Askey's third pantomime for producer Fred Clements, having previously appeared in Leicester and Sheffield. At the former, he played the Opera House in *Dick Whittington*, also appearing as Cheeky Sammy. (He may also have appeared in *Sinbad* in Plymouth as early as 1927.) He finished at the Theatre Royal on Saturday, February 2, and the next night appeared at a concert party in Hastings. Little wonder that Askey was hailed at the time as one of the busiest entertainers in the country.

On December 26, 1937, Askey made television history, appearing with Cyril Fletcher at the BBC's Alexandra Palace studios in *Dick Whittington and His Cat*, the first pantomime to be televised, and a pantomime which producer Cecil Madden claimed was actually written by Askey.

Jack and Jill was described, erroneously, as Askey's first pantomime appearance — he had been absent from the pantomime scene for a number of years — when Askey starred at the Prince of Wales Theatre, Birmingham, for the 1939/1940 season, an eighteen week run. He played the character of "Big-Hearted Arthur." Others in the cast — Billy "Almost a Gentleman" Bennett, Marjorie Appleton, The O'Gorman Brothers — are totally forgotten today. *Jack and Jill* was written, devised, rehearsed, and presented by Emile Littler, which just about guaranteed it would be a box-office and critical success. It also provided him with the opportunity to cast his wife, Cora Griffin, as principal boy.[10] The *Birmingham Daily Gazette* (December 27, 1939) was entranced by Askey's performance, noting, "His small body seems packed with energy, and, flitting about the stage like the busy bee of which he sings, his every movement is a cause for laughter." Forty minutes of the pantomime was broadcast live by the BBC on January 3, 1940 at 8:30 p.m.

Askey also took time out while in Birmingham to participate on December 11, 1939 in the re-opening of the Aston Hippodrome (located in a suburb of the city) after a disastrous fire in February 1938.

For the 1940/1941 season, Arthur starred again in *Jack and Jill* at the Grand Theatre, Leeds. He was back in Leeds in 1947/1948 for *Cinderella* at the Empire Theatre.

(During the war years, with the blackout, it was not uncommon for performances to be given at unusual times. On one week in Leeds, there was a morning show, with the evening performance beginning at 5:00 p.m.)

Askey, under the management of Jack Hylton (who had purchased the pantomime from Emile Littler) brought *Jack and Jill* and a new principal boy Florence Desmond to London's Palace Theatre for the 1941/1942 season. On March 3, 1942, the then Queen Elizabeth took her children, Elizabeth and Margaret, to see the pantomime and the Royal Family helped in the singing of "Hey, Little Hen." The Queen noted how important it was to have good shows at the theatres to help people have some relief from the war.

The following year, as Askey recalled,

"They came to His Majesty's Theatre, where we were doing the same pantomime, and we went up to the Royal Box…and the Queen Mother, the Queen as she was then, said: 'Do you remember, Mr. Buttons, last year you made your entrance in a laundry basket? The children pulled you on and you took the lid up and stood up.' I said, 'Yes.' She said: 'They did that this year in their pantomime at Windsor Castle.' — And the two young princesses looked as if they'd knocked my gags off, you know. They both went like this [he puts his hand to his mouth in a gasp of shock]."[11]

Joining Askey for the 1941/1942 season of *Jack and Jill* was Monsewer Eddie Gray, who he described as the funniest comedian he had ever met or worked with.[15] One of Gray's extra-mural stunts was to step up to a pillar box and start a conversation through the letter slot, asking, "Well how did you get in there in the first place?," and promising to call the fire brigade. By the time Gray moved on, a substantial crowd had gathered.

Monsewer Eddie Gray (1898-1969) is totally forgotten today. Aside from his solo performances, he was often a member of the Crazy Gang, a comedic group that included Flanagan and Allen. As part of the Crazy Gang, and also solo, he was noted for his pathetic attempts to speak in French and a large and fake handlebar moustache.

Askey returned for the 1942/1943 season in *Jack and Jill* at His Majesty's Theatre in London. The principal boy was Kathleen Moody, who was later to marry impresario Lew Grade. Grade became a close friend to the comedian. He was famous for his love of a good cigar, and Eric Morecambe would tell the story,

"Arthur went to see Lew Grade the other day. He was dressed in his brown suit, with brown shoes and a brown shirt and tie. When Lew saw him, he picked him up, put him in his mouth, and lit him."

While appearing in 1943/1944 along with Evelyn Laye in *Cinderella*, Askey was heard in a thirty-minute excerpt on the BBC on January 13, 1944.

The comedian appeared as Buttons — "my favorite pantomime role"[12] — in *Cinderella* at the London Casino in 1947/1948 and for the 1950/1951 season, he was back at the London Casino with *Goody Two Shoes*, with daughter Anthea in the title role, and Askey's sharing comedy routines with legendary circus clown Charlie Cairoli, "set free to abound in their own sense of fun and frolic," according to *The Tatler* (January 10, 1951). Criticism was, of course, pretty much unthinkable. As the *Daily Herald* (November 20, 1950) noted, "Pantomime is the only branch of show business which is no gamble. Cynics may sneer but the public never fails to support a good panto."

Arthur always welcomed pantomime engagements in the London area in that it meant not only could he enjoy entertaining audiences on a nightly basis but also he could live at home.

As Big Hearted Martha, nurse to the babes while they are resident in the sheriff of Nottingham's castle, he could be seen in *Babes in the Wood* at the Brighton Hippodrome for the 1952/1953 season. In the same role, he appeared at London's Golders Green Hippodrome in 1954/1955, with Sally Ann Howes, and went South of the River Thames the following year to play the Streatham Hill Palace, with Patricia Burke as Robin Hood. Askey was back at Streatham Hill in 1959/1960, playing Idle Jack in *Dick Whittington*, with Eve Lister in the title role.

In 1956/1957, Arthur joined forces with daughter Anthea for *Humpty Dumpty* at the Golders Green Hippodrome; he played Dame Clara Crumpett, with Anthea in the title role. Lupino Lane as Umah helped with the comedy. One hour of the show was televised by I.T.V. on December 20, 1956. Askey was back at the Golders Green Hippodrome for the 1958/1959 season, starring as Idle Jack in *Dick Whittington*. The Dame was played by Eddie Molloy.

In 1957/1958, Askey was co-starring at the London Palladium, with pop singer David Whitfield in the title role of *Robinson Crusoe*. Crusoe had a tattoo on his chest showing a map of the pirate treasure, assuring that Whitfield could take off his shirt to the delight of his many female fans. Whitfield obviously considered the part his own, and when he was contracted to appear in *Robinson Crusoe* at the Grand Theatre,

Wolverhampton, in 1966, he was so outraged to discover the role had been given to Janet Brown that he left the production.[13]

Askey played Big Hearted Martha, a landlady from Hull (David Whitfield's home city), and he was helped in the laughs department by fellow comic, Tommy Cooper, described as a "kind of magician," released from a dusty bottle after 200 years.

The critic for *The Stage* (January 2, 1958) was ecstatic in his praise for Askey and Cooper:

"These two, gloriously funny in their own ways, rescue the show from becoming a spectacular musical, and put it right back into the realms of pantomime again whenever they appear. Mr. Askey, as dainty a landlady as one could wish to meet, flirts gaily with the sailors in Panama, jostles energetically with Blackbeard, the Pirate King (played menacingly by Francis de Wolff), copes with the avalanche of fish which hits him during his sojourn inside a whale, dances happily in the arms of a baboon, and returns to England in time to join in a rousing chorus about the virtues of Hull.

"Mr. Cooper takes his part with great seriousness and concentration until something inevitably goes wrong with what he is doing, and then dissolves into maniacal laughter. Undoubtedly he is one of the hits of the show, his characterization and his comedy being as absurd as they are amusing, as bizarre as they are brilliant."

There is an interesting comparison in techniques between Askey and Cooper. Just as Tommy Cooper's efforts at comedy always failed and he found humor in the failure, so did Arthur Askey take delight when a gag went wrong. His joy at what might have been a disaster to any other comedian endeared him to the audience, which similarly found pleasure in calamity.

The London Palladium pantomime ended badly for Askey in that he developed what was initially diagnosed as acute laryngitis. For a while, it seemed as if Askey's voice was totally destroyed, but thanks to a specialist he was coaxed back to full vocal strength.

It was back to the Golders Green Hippodrome in 1961/1962 for *Cinderella*, playing Buttons. "There is surely no more beneficial example of type-casting," wrote *The Stage*. "He looks the part, he lives the part, and the atmosphere of pantomime is that most likely to provoke the unique spirit of fun that bubbles within him."

In 1963/1964, Askey made his first appearance in pantomime in Coventry, starring in *Robin Hood* at the Coventry Theatre, with fellow comedians, Mike and Bernie Winters, playing the robbers, dancer Anton

Dolin, and Mark Wynter in the title role. Mark Wynter was a minor pop star compared to Cliff Richard, with whom Askey appeared in *Aladdin* at the London Palladium for the 1964/1965 season. "Askey is a magnificent, if miniscule, dame," wrote *The Stage* (January 7, 1965), "using to the full his extraordinary gift of instantaneously turning a muffed line into a witty ad-lib."

A portion of the script for this production of *Aladdin* survives, and Arthur's comments on his first entrance are well worth recording, particularly as they typify the pantomime mood:

"You wouldn't think I had a grown-up son would you? No, I can hardly believe it myself. Isn't Nature marvelous?....No, Aladdin's my boy, bless him. And he's just like his father. Except his father didn't sing, He hummed a little. Well, you see, by profession he was a porter in the Fish Market. Everywhere he went he was accompanied by a swarm of bluebottles. So embarrassing on our honeymoon in a strange bed. Terribly shy man he was. When first he saw me in my nylon nightie he made me go and put an apron on....But I miss him. I've got an electric blanket but it isn't the same."

The pantomime, with Askey and Cliff Richard, was revived by the independent television network, Associated Rediffusion on Christmas Day, 1967, in a ninety-minute version.

For the 1965/1966 season, Arthur was again at the Palladium in *Babes in the Wood*, joined by comic Sid James, best remembered for the "Carry On" films, and Australian pop singer, Frank Ifield.

In 1966/1967, he was co-starring with Roy Castle in *Babes in the Wood* at the Wimbledon Theatre. Singer Lulu joined the two comedians.

The comedian was back at the Palladium for the 1967/1968 season appearing again in *Robinson Crusoe*, with pop singer Engelbert Humperdinck in the title role, although his appearances were diminished as a result of a fall through a trap-door that led to Askey's being hospitalized and suffering a heart attack. Understudy Bill Tasker deputized for the comedian; he had earlier worked with Askey in the 1960 television series, *Arthur's Treasured Volumes*.

"I had to decide whether to sue for a nice sum and sit on my bottom in a bungalow in Broadstairs for the rest of my life, or to keep on working," Askey reminisced. He chose the latter, retained his goodwill with the Palladium management and continued performing at the theatre.

Askey returned again to the Palladium the following season for *Jack and the Beanstalk*, playing the mother of Jimmy Tarbuck, as Jack. "I do wonder now and again whether Arthur Askey's script is exactly as it came from the typewriter," pondered one critic.

Comedians Roy Hudd and Arthur Haynes joined Askey for *The Sleeping Beauty* at the Wimbledon Theatre for 1969/1970 season. For a change, not particularly welcomed by the audience, he played the King rather than the Dame.

The 1970/1971 season saw Askey at the Manchester Opera House in *Cinderella*, with comedian Peter Butterworth and Lonnie Donnegan, the "King of Skiffle."

In 1971/1972 and 1972/1973, Askey starred, as Baron Hardup, with Dickie Henderson in *Cinderella* at the Theatre Royal, Nottingham, and the Birmingham Hippodrome respectively. Askey was reunited in 1975/1976 with Dickie Henderson, along with Mark Wynter, for *Babes in the Wood* at the Bristol Hippodrome. Henderson and Askey continued their applause-winning double act in *Babes in the Wood* at the Manchester Palace for the 1976/1977 season. In 1973/1974, Arthur starred at the Richmond Theatre in *Babes in the Wood*, which featured broadcaster Ed Stewart and actress/comedienne Lynda Baron.

After completing a cruise and providing cabaret on the *M.S. Blenheim*, Arthur was booked into the Richmond Theatre for the 1977/1978 pantomime season, starring in *Jack and the Beanstalk*, with Leslie Crowther and Dennis Ramsden. In 1979/1980, Askey was again at the Richmond Theatre in *Dick Whittington*, and writing in *The Guardian* (December 22, 1979), Michael Billington noted, "It would be hard to imagine a more delightful pantomime." He made his last appearance in pantomime at the Richmond Theatre in 1981/1982.

Age did not diminish Askey's work in pantomime nor did it seem to limit his popularity. For the 1978/1979 season, he was starring, as Martha Trot, along with Leslie Crowther, Mark Wynter and Jimmy Edwards, in *Jack and the Beanstalk* at the Alexandra Theatre, Birmingham. There were four matinees and six evening performances a week, and so popular was the show that it was extended well into 1979, with a final performance on March 3rd.

"He is still, in my opinion, one of the best pantomime dames," wrote *The Stage* critic, "with a gentle, sprightly humour which doesn't blare vulgarity but is full of mischievous fun."

The December 1980 pantomime season began without the presence of Arthur Askey. He was forced to cancel his appearance in *Jack and the Beanstalk* in Eastbourne owing to a severe attack of shingles. It was particularly sad for Arthur in that joining him on stage was to be daughter Anthea as a comic fairy. It was the first time in fifty-six years that he had not appeared in a pantomime. "Being in panto is like breathing in and out to me," he commented. "It's a hard chore, but I really enjoy it."[14]

Arthur Askey brought his brand of panto to a wider audience on January 29 1967, when Associated British Corp. presented *Aladdin and His Wonderful Lamp* on commercial television. Joining Arthur were Roy Castle as Wishee Washee and baritone Ian Wallace as The Emperor. Askey, of course, was Widow Twanky. The script was by David Croft, who was to go on and co-script some of the most famous shows on British television, *Dad's Army*, *Are You Being Served?* and *'Allo 'Allo*.

Royal Command Performances

Askey's first royal command performance might well be identified as the March 1942 presentation of *Jack and Jill*, attended by the then-Queen and her two daughters. On June 20 of that year, Arthur was invited to Buckingham Palace to appear before the entire royal family, with his fellow and sister performers, including Bebe Daniels and Ben Lyon, Leslie Henson, Stanley Holloway, Jessie Matthews, Donald Peers, Anne Shelton, Jack Train, the Western Brothers, and Elsie and Doris Water. Writer/Director Val Guest served as compere.

In February 1948, Arthur helps Olsen and Johnson celebrate their London visit and a performance at the Casino.

In all, Askey took part in nine Royal Variety Command Performances, in 1946, 1948, 1952, 1954, 1955, 1957, 1968, and 1972, all at the London Palladium, and also in 1955 at the Opera House, Blackpool. For the last performance, the entire cast was taken to Blackpool by special train from London's Euston Station, and returned to London early the following morning. Among those participating were Eddie Fisher and Debbie Reynolds, George Formby, Norman Evans, and Wilfred Pickles. On June 22, 1977, Askey participated in a Royal Gala Performance at the Alhambra Theatre, Bradford, in the presence of H.R.H. Princess Anne. A 1956 Royal Command Performance, headlined by Liberace, was planned, but cancelled because of the Suez Crisis.

Typical of the response of the Royal Family to Askey was at the first Command Performance in 1946, with Princesses Elizabeth and Margaret leading the applause even before he came on stage. "No more turn was more loudly applauded," reported *The Stage* (November 7, 1946) in a cast that also included Terry-Thomas, Tessie O'Shea and Sid Field. Arthur was certainly immensely proud of his appearances, and very much aware of the honor of being such a frequent guest at a Royal Command Performance, and after the 1954 engagement he took an advertisement in *The Stage* (November 4, 1954) announcing that he was "Very Honoured and Deeply Grateful to All Concerned."

"We like you," Queen Elizabeth told Askey after the 1955 Royal Variety Performance, "You always seem to be enjoying yourself."

The Kid from Stratford

After *Follow the Girls*, there was a relatively short gap before another musical was offered to Arthur. The authors were Barbara Gordon and Basil Thomas (who had been responsible for several of Askey's songs, including "The Death Watch Beetle," "The Pixie" and "The Budgerigar"), with music by Manning Sherwin. The concept for *The Kid from Stratford* was that Arthur had found an old iron box in his uncle's garden in Stratford-on-Avon, and inside it was a musical comedy written by William Shakespeare. As the critic in *The Sketch* (October 27, 1948) explained, "the plot is hard to follow: it is extremely plain if only you will persuade yourself that nothing whatever means anything." As to the star of *The Kid from Stratford*:

"Askey is one of the most ingratiating comedians we have. True, he is not one for your ingenuities and finer elaborations. He is far from subtle. All he seems to do is dart on, blandly mercurial, and frisk about the stage like a wire-haired terrier or the pride of the Upper Fourth organising charades….Askey, bouncing around with the energy of a fourteen-year-old, takes the audience into partnership. Beaming through his horn-rims, he flicks a confidential whisper over the footlights. Presently we are in the show. Under the benevolent hypnotism of the eyes behind those firm-glued spectacles we are content to accept practically any piece of nonsense Askey proposes."

The Kid from Stratford opened at the Princes Theatre on September 29, 1948, transferring to the Winter Garden on December 13, and running for 234 performances through April 23, 1949. It had previewed in Manchester at the Palace Theatre, beginning on August 10, 1948 and then moved on to Edinburgh and Birmingham. The supporting cast, who mattered little, included Ginette Wander, Gil Johnson, Jmmy Godden, Lynette Ray, Chic Elliott, and Mako the Monkey. Towards the end of the run, daughter Anthea took over a small part in the show. Henry Thomas directed, and Jack Waller presented after Jack Hylton had rejected the show.

Australia and *The Love Racket*

After the closure of *The Kid from Stratford*, Askey considered taking it to Australia for his first visit there, but eventually decided to revive *The Love Racket*. In November 1949, he, May and Anthea boarded the *S.S. Strathmore*, with Roy Royston and Valerie Tandy from the original cast and newcomers, Rae Johnson and Audrey Jeans. Following stops in Bombay, Ceylon, Perth, and Adelaide, the company left the boat in Melbourne on November 24, 1949.

The Love Racket opened in Melbourne at the Tivoli Theatre on Christmas Eve, 1949, and ran for six months, followed by one month in Brisbane, four months in Sydney, closing the first week of October 1950, and ten days at the Theatre Royal, Adelaide.

The Melbourne run was intended to be for only four months, but such was Askey's popularity that it was extended. Even the Australian Prime Minister, Robert Menzies, went to see Askey at the Tivoli, on Australia Day no less, January 30, 1950. On opening night, after the play was ended, Askey returned to the stage for a further fifteen minutes of jokes, and "had the entire theatre waiting on his every word. Surely a great tribute to the command he holds over his audience." One newspaper critic wrote,

"Not since Tommy Trinder has the Tivoli given us such a likable and lively personality. Mr. Askey scored an immediate and pronounced success….Who could tire of Arthur Askey, the diminutive comedian who romps through every scene as if he created it as he went."[16]

Askey also found time to star in a television series, *The Arthur Askey Show*, supported by Anthea, which aired on Sunday evenings, beginning February 12, 1950, and was last aired on July 7, 1950.

Arthur and Anthea returned to England on the *S.S. Stratheden* in time for rehearsals for yet another pantomime, *Goody Two Shoes*, at the London Casino. The visit to Australia had intended to last only six months, but ultimately Askey and Anthea stayed almost a year there.

Bet Your Life

No sooner was *Goody Two Shoes* over than Arthur was presented with a new musical project by Jack Hylton titled *Bet Your Life*, written by Alan Melville, with music and lyrics by Kenneth Leslie Smith and Charles Zwar, and with American Julie Wilson and Sally Ann Howes as the female leads and with Brian Reece in support, which went into rehearsals in August 1951. Askey's character was that of a jockey who dreamt up winners in his sleep; at least he had the right stature although he was definitely no supporter of horse racing.

After watching the Grand National, which has horses jumping over thirty fences for two laps of the Aintree Racecourse just outside of Liverpool, Askey writes in his autobiography that he would like to throw a saddle over Mrs. Mirabel Topham, the owner of the racecourse, and ride her over the fences.[17]

Bet Your Life opened at the New Theatre, Oxford on December 4, 1951, and then went on to the Manchester Opera House for the Christmas season. The show came to the London Hippodrome on February 18, 1952, and ran for 363 performances. The director was Richard Bird, whose next London production was to be *Call Me Madam*. The unidentified critic in the *Daily Sketch* (February 27, 1952) wrote,

"Fevered is the word. The cast rackets through with so much vigour that the plot could be wilder than it is, and, believe me, that would be difficult."

"The show is bright and brisky," reported *The Stage* (February 21, 1952), "and it has qualities that, on the whole, should ensure success." This comment despite some booing from areas of the audience on opening night, which Arthur, in his autobiography, blames on audience agitation at a show that had gone on despite the recent death of the King, but which seems more to have been directed at the comedian himself. On June 12, Noele Gordon replaced Julie Wilson, and the following day, *Bet Your Life* began twice nightly performances.

The Love Match

While appearing in pantomime in Brighton for the 1952-1953 season, Askey saw a play titled *Just My Bill*, starring Thora Hird, Leo Franklyn, Danny Ross, and author Glenn Melvyn. He decided it would be an ideal vehicle for him in the upcoming summer season in Blackpool. Producer Jack Hylton and director Richard Bird agreed, and *Just My Bill* became *The Love Match*, which was to prove a healthy and long-running vehicle for Arthur, particularly after he had excised most of the love interest and some political commentary.

Daughter Anthea joined the cast, and *The Love Match* opened for a one-week engagement at the New Theatre, Oxford, before beginning its summer run in Blackpool. Jack Hylton was so taken with the play that, after a two-week presentation at the Palace Theatre, Manchester, he brought it to London's West End and the Palace Theatre on October 11, 1953. The London critics were lukewarm at best, but emphasized that this was a comedy intended primarily for less-sophisticated Northern audiences, admittedly a somewhat patronizing response. *The Times* (November 11, 1953), utilizing football jargon, described the play as "a good clean game, and will probably be a drawer." The veteran critic W.A. Darlington in the *Daily Telegraph* (November 11, 1953) described *The Love Match* as "just a frolic." *The Stage* (November 12, 1953), wrote that *The Love Match* was "by no means a disgrace to the light entertainment on hire in the West End at the moment."

In complete disagreement, and very much speaking his mind, was Kenneth Tynan, whom Askey obviously disliked and refers to in his autobiography as "that failed actor" ("Shakespeare with a stutter"). In the *Daily Sketch* (November 11, 1952), Tynan wrote,

"Weep, theatre-lovers, for the die is cast. There is a corner of a London street which is for ever Blackpool.

"*The Love Match*…may now be pointed out to visitors as proof that provincial taste has a stronghold in London.

"Or perhaps stranglehold is the word I want. Before long, no doubt, we shall have concert parties at the Criterion and Frank Randle [an atrociousy unfunny Northern comedian] at Drury Lane. The die is cast, and the cast, to put it bluntly, is death.

"A provincial myself, I'm in no position to be priggish; it's simply that *The Love Match*, advertised as 'a laughter show,' failed to make me laugh. But underlying its arrival in London I detect a sinister assumption — that the West End is no longer the arbiter of theatrical taste.

"Few managements nowadays quarrel with popular demand, but most of them at least give the Londoner what he wants, not what somebody else wanted. The new attitude, implied by *The Love Match*, seems to be: 'Let them eat Eccles cakes.'

"And so, out of exile, a procession of 30-year-old gags and catchphrases come trooping back,"

After six months at the Palace, *The Love Match* moved to the Victoria Palace with Lupino Lane replacing Askey for seven weeks, beginning July 26, 1954, while he starred in a film version. (In March/April of that year, Glenn Melvyn was ill and replaced by Leo Franklyn.) Askey was also replaced in the touring version of *The Love Match* — beginning November 1, 1954 by Yorkshire-born Bunny Doyle.

One prominent member of *The Love Match* company was stage manager William Stewart. He and Anthea Askey fell in love and married on her birthday in 1956 at All Souls Church, Langham Place, London. It was a happy marriage, sadly ending in divorce, and produced four children, Jane, Andrew, William, and, the first, James William, who died on October 21, 1959, following an emergency operation less than a month after his birth.

Daughter Jane recalls,

"They were blissfully happy and very much in love. Dad often told me mum used to sing and dance around the house, and we had a very happy and sometimes quite magical childhood, although strict. However, things deteriorated when we moved from London to Sussex (I was nine, Will just born and mum very frail after a very difficult birth where she had a fifty percent chance of survival). Mum also lost a lot of good friends, and saw far less of granddad who used to live at the bottom of our road in London, and she also had less contact with 'theatre people' (and didn't get on with dad's 'TV people'). Dad also lost his studio just before we left London and had to sell insurance to support us when we moved to Sussex, and it took him time to rebuild his business, and a lot of time to grow it, so mum was on her own a lot…and that's when problems really started. They eventually couldn't live with each other but never fell out of love, as is borne out by them continuing to see each other, chatting on the phone, and often having dinner together, right to the end of their lives."[18]

An actress almost from childhood, making her radio debut in a sitcom based on the "Just William" books in 1948 at the age of fifteen, Anthea had the problem of a famous father who obviously helped advance her career, and to a large extent she was dismissed as her father's daughter, always to be found in anything in which he starred, rather than a competent actress and singer in her own right. "I am a very unambitious person," she once remarked, "I have never wanted to be a star or a big name."[19] She was always Arthur Askey's daughter, and he was devoted to her. On Anthea's 21st birthday, her father hosted a party at the Dorchester Hotel, where guests included Richard Murdoch, Norman Wisdom, the entire Crazy Gang, including, of course, Monsewer Eddie Gray, and Anthea's "secret love," actor Herbert Lom.

Arthur and daughter Anthea on her wedding day.

In later years, Anthea appeared on stage with Will Fyffe, Jr., the pianist son of the Scottish comedian, and they may have been vaguely discussing wedding plans, but this seems nothing more than giving Anthea something to focus on, to try and help her beat the developing cancer. No wedding was ever arranged. Sadly, Anthea died of cancer in Worthing on February 28, 1999.

What a Racket!

Writing of summer entertainment in Blackpool, *The Stage* (August 3, 1961) commented,

"The pattern for the season play at the Grand is now well-established: it must have a north country setting, contain plenty of situations permitting of broad humour, have a good leavening of sheer knockabout, and allow its comedian scope enough to display his special line of comedy. Success depends on the audience being able to identify themselves with one or other of the characters."

Such a play was Dennis Spencer's *What a Racket!*, a slice of Lancashire life, which opened at the King's Theatre, Southsea, on May 1, 1961, en route to Blackpool. The characters consisted of the browbeaten father, played by Arthur, his bossy but good-natured wife, played by Betty Driver, his granny, played by Beatrice Varley, and a rock 'n' roll singer, played by Bunny May. The plot was slight and the play had already been produced earlier under the title of *Rock Bottom*.

On July 7, 1961, the BBC broadcast a forty-five minute version of the play with the orginal cast. *What a Racket!* subsequently toured with Jessie Matthews replacing Betty Driver. One wonders how serviceable would have been her Lancashire accent.

Outside of pantomime and summer seasons, Askey was tireless in his stage appearances. "The old routine," as he would call it. Year in and year out, he was always performing be it at the Hippodrome, Brighton in March 1948 with the Western Brothers, the Grand Theatre, Derby in June 1949, Winter Gardens, Eastbourne in August 1949; A frequent comedic companion on stage was the above-mentioned Monsewer Eddie Gray — at the Coventry Hippodrome in May 1948 and the Winter Gardens, Morecambe, in June 1951. Askey had been at the Coventry Hippodrome on December 5, 1943, appearing with Tommy Handley and His ITMA Gang in a charity performance for the C.E.T. Parcels Fund and Shipwrecked Mariners. He would often complain that the traveling was more tiring than the actual performances. Perhaps because of this, he spent the entire summer of 1950 headlining at the Imperial Theatre, Brighton, in *High Tide*, along with Florence Desmond, Peter Butterworth, and, as might be expected, Monsewer Eddie Gray, the high spot of which was a parody of *Forever Amber*. Askey headlined at the Coventry Hippodrome, supported by Roy Castle and Yana, for the theatre's 23rd birthday show, opening October 17, 1960.[20] It was not until March 15, 1953, that Askey made his first appearance in Preston — in a Grand Charity Concert.

The content of many of the one-evening performances would vary substantially depending on the situation. For example, on Easter Sunday, April 18, 1954, he appeared at the Winter Garden, Eastbourne, with a group of classical artists, including solo violinist and pianist, a baritone, and a soprano. In fact, during the 1950s, Arthur appeared on a regular basis in more serious presentations under the title of "Music for the Millions," produced by Harold Fielding.

1. A reference to the police raiding dancing classes at which the partners were considered to be moving too closely together.
2. Arthur Askey, *Before Your Very Eyes*, p. 138.
3. Horace Richards, "I Thang Yow!"
4. Jim Hiley, "Revolution in Pantoland," p. 15.
5. "Askey's Impression…of the Australian Theatre."
6. Ibid.
7. "Cryer the Beloved Stand-up Comedian," p. 19.
8. Simon Blumenfeld, "There's Nothing Like a Dame," p. 10.
9. "The Pantomime Tradition," p. 12.
10. Emile Littler (1903-1985) was a member of a legendary theatrical family that included brother Prince and sister Blanche. From the 1930s through the 1950s, Emile Little's pantomimes dominated Britain's entertainment scene. He was knighted in 1974.
11. Russell Harty, *Russell Harty Plus*, p. 168.
12. Arthur Askey, *Before Your Very Eyes*, p. 148.
13. David Whitfield (1925-1980) had begun his working life as a laborer in his native Hull. He enjoyed fame thanks to a hit recording of "Cara Mia," and his fan base included both mothers and teenage girls. His career suffered a major setback in October 1966 when he was found guilty of exposing himself in front of an eleven-year-old girl, although he was found innocent of a more serious charge, that of sexually assaulting the girl. In 2012, the city of Hull unveiled a statue in his memory.
14. Quoted in the *Liverpool Echo*, December 22, 1980, p. 2.

15. Arthur Askey, *Before Your Very Eyes,* p. 125.

16. Quoted in *The Stage,* February 2, 1950, p. 8.

17. Arthur Askey, *Before Your Very Eyes,* p. 160.

18. Jane Stewart to Anthony Slide, e-mail dated March 12, 2020.

19. Fred Norris, "My Dad…Oh How I miss Him," p. 6.

20. While in Coventry, Askey took time out on November 8, 1960, to open the Fryer Tuck and serve some fresh-cooked pies (baked in a rotary oven, supposedly the first in the world).

Arthur demonstrates his affinity with the television camera.

CHAPTER SIX

On Television

While he might have been a regular on television for decades, indeed since its experimental phase in the 1930s, surprisingly Arthur Askey had no great liking for the medium:

"John Logie Baird, the man who invented television. Curse the feller! Killed the theatres — which I prefer of course to telly. I like live entertainment."[1]

Arthur Askey may not have liked television, but he certainly embraced it once it had supplanted radio as the medium of choice for most Britishers. There were two fifteen minute programs, *Starlight*, in which he appeared in August and September 1951. The second show was broadcast from the annual radio show at London's Earls Court on September 7, 1951, and the following night Arthur again traveled to Earls Court to headline in a seventy-five minute program, *Holiday Camp*.

On Christmas Day, from 1951 through 1954, the BBC presented a live *Television Christmas Party*, hosted the first year by Leslie Mitchell and Jerry Desmonde, and then by McDonald Hobley. Featured stars included the popular husband-and-wife singing team of Anne Ziegler and Webster Booth, and comedians Ethel Revnell and Gracie West, Jimmy Jewel and Ben Warris, Norman Wisdom, Tommy Cooper, and Terry-Thomas. One year, either 1951 or 1952, the last was too drunk to appear and Askey substituted, showing a natural affinity for the television camera to which he would speak directly, sticking his face in the camera and asking the audience to count his freckles. He was a television natural, and the BBC's head of light entertainment, Ronnie Waldman, was quick to acknowledge this.

As June Whitfield, who worked often with Askey, recalled,

"He was wonderfully natural in front of the camera and not remotely daunted by it. He spoke into the lens as if he was having an inconsequential chat with a friend. He said, 'I don't think about the millions watching. I just image two people sitting at home eating their dinner in front of the telly.'"[2]

When things went wrong, he would draw attention to them, rather than try to cover them up, letting the viewer become an intimate and integral part of the presentation. On a desert set for a parody of *Beau Geste*, he would walk to the edge of the set, commenting, "Fancy the desert finishing here." If he was late with his entrance, he would turn to the camera, commenting, "I'll be with you in a minute playmates." When the stage manager indicated that extra dialogue, etc. was to be added as the show was running early, Arthur would again turn to the camera, telling his audience, "You're lucky. You're getting an extra bit." He would ad-lib so much that the show would now be running over, resulting in his having to tell the camera/viewing audience, "He's hurrying us up now." There was a deliberately unrehearsed atmosphere on the set, and that was what most appealed to the audience both in the studio and at home.

"As usual I was a pioneer and did all my best work then, or before people knew any better," recalled Askey.[3]

Before Your Very Eyes

His catch phrase, "Before Your Very Eyes" was adopted as the title for a series of variety-style shows starring Askey and airing as three fifteen-minute programs on Sunday evenings in April and May 1952, six thirty-minute programs on Wednesday evenings in February through April 1953, and five thirty-minute programs on Friday evenings in February through April 1955. According to Askey, their popularity was on a par with that enjoyed back in the lte 1930s by *Band Waggon*.

The shows were authored by Sid Colin and Talbot Rothwell. Each consisted of an introduction, followed by three sketches. Askey, of course, dominated, but for series two he was joined by Diana Decker and Dickie Henderson.

Diana Decker was actually born in Hollywood, but moved as a child to the United Kingdom, where she spent her entire career as an actress and singer. Noted for her roles as a dizzy blonde, she started her screen career during World War Two, but enjoyed her biggest success on television and as a recording artist.

Although born in London, Dickie Henderson (1922-1985) began his career in Hollywood. His father, Dick Henderson, had been a comedian on the vaudeville stage and on screen, and it was perhaps not surprising that when Hollywood needed an English boy the studios turned to Henderson's son Dickie. In 1932, he was cast as the young son of Clive Brook and Diana Wynyard in Noel Coward's *Cavalcade*. Dickie

Henderson's British career began after World War Two. Following *Before Your Very Eyes*, he was starred in his own shows, *The Dickie Henderson Show* (1957-1959), *The Dickie Henderson Half-Hour* (1958-1999), and the sitcom *The Dickie Henderson Show* (1960-1968), all seen on commercial television. He and Arthur were the closest of friends, and Arthur's daughter, Anthea, appeared as Henderson wife in the shows from the 1950s.

There had been a suggestion that Anthea and Henderson were in a relationship, but it seem unlikely, and Askey's grandchildren strongly deny this. Henderson had, in fact, married Dixie Ross of the Ross Sisters, a singing, dancing and contortionist act that gives a truly memorable performance in *Broadway Rhythm* (1944).

Series three is notable for introducing television audiences to Sabrina.

Sabrina

"I wanted a dumb blonde for my series. And I got one," Askey recalled.[4] Her breasts were quite remarkable, so much so that they had and have the capacity to both to startle and transfix. As for her walk, well, while complaining that she didn't know how to walk properly, the comedian noted, "I wish my watch had a movement like that."

The concept of a good-looking, silent, female stooge was not original to Askey. He borrowed the idea from Billy Merson (1879-1947), a Nottingham-born comic of music hall, revue and pantomime, who wrote and introduced the song "The Spaniard That Blighted My Life." Merson would perform a musical act and for no apparent reason a girl sat close by to the musicians reading a book. When the musicians left the stage, the girl continued to sit, reading her book.

Several women were auditioned, and eventually Askey and his producer, Bill Ward settled upon Norma Ann Sykes, with an eyeglass figure of 42.5-inch breasts, an eighteen inch weight and thirty-six inch hips. (The breasts were actually insured for some 100,000 pounds.) In some respects, she was similar to other British blondes such as Diana Dors, Belinda Lee and Shirley Eaton, except they had talent and she did not. Born in Stockport in the North of England in 1936, she was a first rate swimmer, but it was a move with her parents to Blackpool (where they ran a hotel) and a bout with polio that led to her transformation from an overweight teenager to a perfect-sized young woman as she worked out on a regular basis to recover from her illness. At the age of sixteen, Sykes moved to London, and worked as a photographic model, posing nude, but she had no acting experience prior to being hired. The lack of acting talent didn't really matter, as photographer Sydney Aylett pointed out: "She radiated a sort of sensual purity." "I'm using my bust as a jumping off place for bigger and better things," she proclaimed.

It was Askey who renamed Norma Ann Sykes Sabrina. He took the name from the 1954 Audrey Hepburn-William Holden film, *Sabrina*, then playing in the U.K. under the title of *Sabrina Fair*, the title of the

Arthur with Sabrina.

play from which the film is adapted. (In his autobiography, Askey does not reference the film but claims the name came from the stage play then playing at London's Palace Theatre.)

"When I discovered Sabrina — you know with the big boobs and everything," Askey recalled, "the BBC were very chary about what I was going to do with her. But I didn't do anything offensive with her."[5]

Sabrina made her television debut on episode one of the third season of *Before Your Very Eyes*. Rather like Billy Merson's female stooge, in the first episode she just sat on a chair while Askey approached the camera and asked, "I wonder who that is?" In the second episode, she was supposed to speak but somehow failed to perform, and Askey had to tell the audience there was a breakdown in sound. In episode three, Sabrina was speechless because of a chill and was seated with her feet in a mustard bath. In the fourth episode, she was cast as a maid and scheduled to announce, "Breakfast is almost ready." She failed to speak yet again. In the final scene of the episode, which was cut because the show was running over, Sabrina was seen wearing a sarong and tied to a tree with a boiling cauldron in front of her. A cannibal was to appear and announce, "Breakfast is almost ready."

Despite stories to the contrary, and pronouncements that she was forbidden to talk on television, Sabrina did actually speak a few lines in the series. She also began to eclipse Askey as the star, receiving far more fan mail that did he, a situation which apparently amused rather than offended the comedian. Following the television series, Sabrina was seen in three British films, *Stock Car* (1955), *Ramsbottom Rides Again* (1956) and *Blue Murder at St. Trinian's* (1957). She toured in cabaret, visited Australia, and eventually moved to the United States. Basically, as the *Daily Mail* had it, Sabrina was the Kim Kardashian of her day, famous for being famous.

In America, she had small roles in three very minor Hollywood films and was seen in a couple of episodes of the Ron Ely television series, *Tazran* (1967). Sabrina was often described as the British Marilyn Monroe or the British Jayne Mansfield, and ironically she replaced the latter in her penultimate film, *The Ice House*. Sabrina married a wealthy gynecologist, Dr. Harry Meisheimer, in 1967; the marriage ended in divorce in 1974. Tragedy struck when Sabrina had a botched operation for chronic back problems, which left her wheelchair bound. With her looks gone, no career and very little money, the poor woman ended her days in a suburb of Los Angeles renamed Toluca Woods, but formerly a part of North Hollywood. For many years a recluse, she died on November 24, 2016, at the age of eighty. The photographs of her at the end, published in the *Daily Mail* (October 13, 2017) are incredibly sad.

Up until 1954, the BBC had a policy on not permitting variety-type entertainment on Sunday television. It was inappropriate, at least according to "Auntie BBC," and the result was what was described as a dreary pattern of parlour games, plays and piano recitals. But in March of that year, the corporation began asking top performers, such as Frankie Howerd, Terry-Thomas, Norman Wisdom, and Arthur Askey, if they might consider Sunday performances — which, after all, would not compete with weekday stage appearances. "Sunday is the one day we aren't in the theatres. It's sensible, and I'm sure a great many acts would love to appear," commented Arthur.[6] The BBC recognized that if television curmudgeon Gilbert Harding could grumble of Sundays why should not people be allowed to laugh on that day?[7]

It was Jack Hylton, Askey's friend and mentor who was responsible for persuading the comedian to leave the BBC and move to commercial television. When the government, on October 27, 1954, issued the first contract for commercial weekday television in the London area, it was to Associated-Rediffusion (a conglomerate owned by Broadcast Relay Service and Associated Newspapers). The new company hired Jack Hylton as its advisor on Light Entertainment, and Hylton, in turn, created Jack Hylton Television Productions Ltd. to produce programming of one hour every two weeks and thirty minutes every week, beginning in September 1955.[8]

The first Jack Hylton program, broadcast on September 29, 1955, was *Talk of the Town*, with the title taken from his revue then running at the Adelphi Theatre. The cast included old-timers, such as Robb Wilton, Stanley Holloway, and Flanagan and Allen, together with newcomers, including Hylton's latest discovery, Shirley Bassey. "If this is all Mr. Hylton has to offer television he should confine his activities to the live theatre — and, for pity's sake, leave television alone," commented the *Daily Mail* (September 30, 1955).

Love and Kisses

Hylton persevered, while still concentrating on stars of a certain age, and decided to film Arthur Askey's latest stage production, *Love and Kisses*, currently playing in Blackpool. Rather than film in that city, the cast and sets were brought down to London, to the Princes Theatre, where the show was filmed (using four cameras) before an invited audience on Sunday, October 18, 1955. The show was broadcast not as a single night's entertainment, but in five weekly instalment, from November 4 through December 2, 1955. Each episode opened and closed with comments from Arthur Askey. "The thinness of each instalment is padded out with introductory comments by Arthur Askey and the author Glenn Melvyn, which grow sillier every week," commented the *Daily Mail* (November 19, 1955). More enthusiastic was *The Stage* (November 10, 1955), commenting, "The filmed play proved much better than might be expected. The pace was fast, the situations funny."

Viewers in the North of England had the opportunity to see *Love and Kisses* in its entirety, in one broadcast, on December 23, 1966.

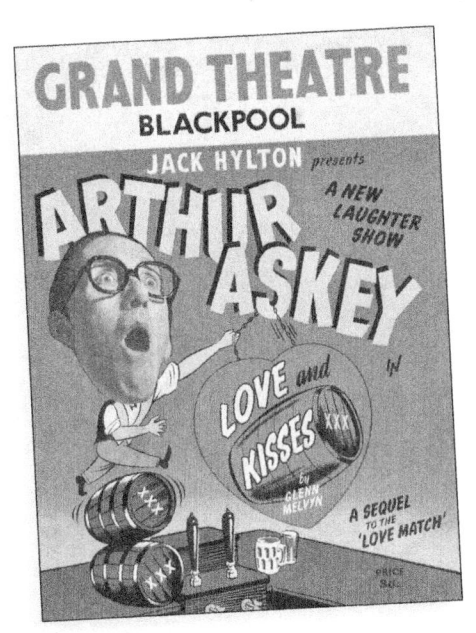

Jack Hylton and Arthur Askey next teamed up with the transfer of *Before Your Very Eyes* from the BBC to commercial television. *Before Your Very Eyes* was broadcast for three series on a weekly basis by Associated-Rediffusion from February 24, 1956 through December 16, 1957.

Joining Askey were daughter Anthea, June Whitfield and, of course, Sabrina. As June Whitfield recalled, "The show consisted of topical sketches in the first half, followed by a longer parody sketch, usually of a film, in part two."[9] She also notes that Associated Rediffusion management was not too happy with Arthur's ad libs which made fun of the medium of television, and he was asked to tone down his off-the-cuff comments.

"No, I haven't quarreled with the BBC," explained Askey to the *Daily Mirror* (January 6, 1956). "It's just that commercial TV has rattled the money-box a little more....To appear every fortnight on television means losing a fortnight's work elsewhere. Commercial TV has made it worth my while"

While *Before Your Very Eyes* was airing, Jack Hylton also celebrated Askey's thirty years in show business with *Arthur's Anniversary*, broadcast on March 15, 1957. It was decidedly old-fashioned entertainment, provided by Askey together with daughter Anthea, Richard Mudoch, Sabrina, Danny Ross, and announcer McDonald Hobley. Askey sang the song he had introduced at his first professional engagement, "Bumpity Bump." "He was in splendid form," reported Antonia Frazer in the *Evening Standard* (March 16, 1957). "Old jokes popped like champagne corks."

In 1956, Arthur Askey discovered that nationwide fame could also be a handicap when he was inadvertently involved in a murder. In May of that year, the partially-clad body of thirty-six year old Mrs. Diana Suttey was discovered near Hemel Hempstead, Hertfordshire. Witnesses described a man seen near the scene who bore a remarkable resemblance to Arthur Askey. The comedian was interviewed by the police, but, of course, was just

Arthur and June Whitfield.

an innocent man who resembled a murderer. Askey laughed the whole thing off, but did appear remarkably unsympathetic towards the victim and her family.

By the end of 1957, it was very obvious that *Before Your Very Eyes* was running out of steam. At the start of the last season, the *Daily Mirror* (November 19, 1957) complained that it had begun "with more gusto than gags…and the show ran out of material well before it ran out of time." At the same time, as viewers would affirm, the *Daily Mirror* noted that Askey was so exuberant and so friendly that "it seemed downright sour not to laugh at him." Ill health also forced the series to be curtailed, coupled with Askey's exorbitant salary of 800 pounds per show and his demands as to which studio should be used.

Jack Hylton continued his association with the Askey family by starring Anthea as the wife of Dickie Henderson in *The Dickie Henderson Show*, broadcast from July 11, 1958, through May 5, 1959. (Dickie Henderson had worked with Jack Hylton and His Band some twenty years earlier.)

Askey continued his association with commercial television, but without Jack Hylton's participation. There was *The Arthur Askey Show* — there seems to have been a lack of originality in naming his programs — produced by Associated Television (ATV) and aired in six, sixty-minute episodes from February 28, 1959 through September 3, 1960.

Arthur's Treasured Volumes

The Arthur Askey Show was followed by *Arthur's Treasured Volumes*, again consisting of six, sixty-minute programs, aired from May 2 through June 6, 1960. The show would begin with daughter Anthea selecting a book from the shelf and describing the plot, which was then dramatized with her father in the lead. None of the volumes were real, published books, with the plots created by writer Dave Freeman. It might perhaps have been better if real books and real plotlines had been utilized. Guest stars included June Whitfield, Wilfred Brambell and Geoffrey Palmer, with regulars Sam Kydd and Arthur Mullard in support of Askey.

Only one episode of *Arthur's Treasured Volumes* was thought to exist until 2019 when the missing episodes were found in the ITV Archives, and all were screened at London's National Film Theatre.

Arthur Mullard also appeared with Askey in the next ATV series, *The Arthur Askey Show*, which aired from March 11 through April 22, 1961. The new series was set in 1910, with Askey playing cockney Arthur Pilbeam and June Whitfield appearing as his wife, Emily. Audiences may well have found it odd that Arthur's television wife was young enough to be his daughter. Arthur Mullard played neighbor Mr. Rossiter, with his wife played by Patricia Hayes. Dave Freeman was again the writer. "There seem to be many opportunities for a good laugh at the expense of the old-fashioned way of life, but they weren't exploited to the full," complained *The Stage* (March 16, 1961). "Somehow the show did not really come up to expectations." There was a general feeling that producer Jack Hylton was skimping on the budget.

Six additional episodes were apparently filmed, but they were never broadcast.

Raise Your Glasses

Arthur Askey's television career was far from over at this time. In 1962, from October 14 through December 16, he co-starred with Alan Melville, who also wrote the show, in the series, *Raise Your Glasses*, which featured various reveue-style sketches and took its title from the fact that both stars wore glasses. "It was not a world-shattering success, but we enjoyed doing it," remembered Askey.[10] The show was also featured as part of the BBC's *Christmas Night with the Stars*, broadcast on December 25, 1962. On March 8, 1967, Askey appeared as himself, reminiscing about his career on the BBC's *Suddenly It's...* series.

Alan Melville did not agree with Askey's assessment of *Raise Your Glasses*, writing in his autobiography,

"We were, in fact, a disaster. The millions who adore Arthur (myself included) bitterly resented me looming around in a dinner-jacket looking podgily po-faced; my three fans were furious when Arthur did one of his funny walks or said 'ay thenk yew' a full two inches from the camera just when I was being tremendously witty."[11]

Raise Your Glasses was to be Askey's last major television series. His television career did not exactly end, but it began to consist more of celebrity appearances on popular shows such as *Celebrity Squares*, *The Generation Game* and *Juke Box Jury*.

Askey was one of the first featured celebrities on Melville's long-running BBC series, *Alan Melville Takes You from A to Z*, which went through the alphabet a couple of times over its four year run from 1956 through 1959.

Surprisingly, Arthur appeared not as himself but as music hall comedian Billy Merson in *Ninety Years On*, celebrating the 90th birthday of Winston Churchill and televised in November 1964, on his birthday eve. Noel Coward hosted the show, written by Terence Rattigan, which also featured Cicely Courtneidge, Jimmy Edwards, Roy Castle, and Ian Carmichael. Presumably as a Conservative, Askey took some delight in appearing in a program honoring the greatest of all Conservative Prime Ministers.

A Northern Irish playwright, Sam Cree, had adapted *The Love Match* for Irish audiences. Among Cree's other works was *Second Honeymoon*, set in a seaside boarding house. Askey appeared in a production of the play at the Grand Theatre, Blackpool, in the summer of 1966, and an abbreviated version was televised by the BBC on July 26.

There were somewhat unexpected guest appearances such as in *A Hundred Years of Humphrey Hastings*, a six-part BBC2 series spotlighting the impact of practical science on a Twickenham household, with Dudley Foster in the title role witnessing the impact of practical science on his Twickenham household.. The program was broadcast in November and December of 1967, and Arthur appeared in part five, "1932 — Vision and Sound." Also in 1967, Askey starred in a pilot, *No Strings*, for ABC Television, in which he appeared as a piano tuner. Only the one episode

Arthur's Treasured Volumes, *with daughter Anthea*.

was made and broadcast on January 29, 1967, with a supporting cast including Ann Lancaster, Jack Haig and Bob Todd, and it was never televised to London audiences.

Just as Askey's radio career basically ended with a game show, so did his television career similarly come to a close. For three seasons, from 1970 through 1971, he was one of the guests, along with Ted Ray and others, on Yorkshire Television's production of *Joker's Wild*, hosted by Barry Cryer. The idea was that comedians would be given a subject for a joke and then compete with each other to come up with the best punch line.

As his television career diminished it seemed appropriate to honor the comedian with a celebration on *This Is Your Life*. There were actually two appearances, the most prominent of which took place (or at least was televised) on December 25, 1974, with a cast that included Dickie Henderson, June Whitfield, Cyril Fletcher, Charlie Drake, Jack Warner, Richard Murdoch (on film from South Africa), and, of course, Sabrina. The last looked as if she had had breast reduction and had trouble delivering her one line (which obviously she is trying to remember). The airing of the program of Christmas Day is indicative of Askey's fame and popularity at this point of time.

1. Russell Harty, *Russell Harty Plus*, p. 168.
2. June Whitfield, *...and June Whitfield*, p. 113.
3. Arthur Askey, *Before Your Very Eyes*, p. 165.
4. *Daily Mirror*, January 6, 1956, p. 2.
5. Horace Richards, "Ay Thang Yow!"
6. "The Answers to Frowzy Sundays!," p. 4.
7. Gilbert Harding (1907-1960) was a British radio and television personality best known as a panelist on *What's My Line?* He was an unattractive, exceedingly rude character who hid his homosexuality.
8. The contract was dated July 13, 1955.
9. June Whitfield, *...and June Whitfield*, p. 113.
10. Arhur Askey, *Before Your Very Eyes*, p. 165.
11. Alan Melville, *Merely Melville*, p. 8.

Arthur begins to show his age, in terms of both his gags and his appearance.

CHAPTER SEVEN

Ol' Man Askey

On November 17, 1980, Arthur Askey appeared for what was to be the last time at a Royal Variety Performance, in the presence of the Queen Mother. He stood alone on stage and with typical comedic good humor but with an unusual hint of pathos he sang a parody of "Ol' Man River" from *Show Boat:*

"Ol' man Askey, dat ol' man Askey,
Though somewhat dated, he feels elated,
Rejuvenated, he still keeps rolling along.
He don't get younger, but don't feel older.
There's silver threads now among the golder,
But ol' man Askey, he still keeps rolling along.
Why should he still sweat and strain,
Frequently cracking his gags in vain.
Tell that joke, get no laugh,
Not a blinking soul wants an autograph."

The song is a reminder of the passing years, but through those years, Arthur Askey had never lost his sense of humor, his sense of fun, and nor, for that matter, had he lost his audience. The problem was that, like the comedian, the audience was also getting older — and not being replaced by a younger one.

As wags would have it, Askey soldiered on, telling the same old gags, until, literally, he didn't have a leg to stand on.

He also did not have a wife to lend support. In 1969, May's mental health had started to decline, and she would often be confused, at times not even recognizing Arthur as her husband. "Pre-Senile Dementia" was diagnosed, what would now be labelled Alzheimer's disease. Arthur and Anthea began a search for an appropriate facility for May and eventually found St. George's Retreat in East Sussex. May, "my little wife," as her husband always called her, was there for four years, during which time Arthur and Anthea visited on a regular basis, and the former also organized live stage performances for the residents, with stars including Val Doonican, Vera Lynn, Dickie Henderson (often described as Askey's closest friend), Dora Bryan, and Jack Warner. On April 9, 1974, Arthur learned that his wife had died during the night.

Harry Secombe and Arthur celebrate Vera Lynn's thirty years in show business at a Variety Club event in March 1972.

"So, at the age of seventy-four, my sweetheart from my office days in Liverpool was no more. Her end had been expected for some time, but the blow was just as hard to bear when it happened."[1]

Arthur did what one might expect of him. He went back to performing, working as hard as ever. Daughter Anthea wanted him to come and live with her and her husband in the country, but Askey insisted on staying on in the Kensington flat, where he and May had lived together, and into which sister Rene had moved when the latter went into St. George's Retreat, surrounded by the Chinese Lacquer furniture that May loved. Even Arthur's piano was in that style.

Also in 1969, Askey was made an Officer of the Most Excellent Order of the British Empire (OBE). A decade later, in 1981, he received a CBE

(Commander of the Most Excellent Order of the British Empire), the highest ranking Order of the British Empire Award.

1974 was a year in which Askey celebrated his fiftieth anniversary in show business, and on October 17, the Variety Club hosted a luncheon in his honor. Present were Max Bygraves, Morecambe and Wise, and Arthur Low, best remembered for his work in *Dad's Army*, who hailed Arthur as

With Max Bygraves and Eric Sykes.

"one of the greatest comedians of the century." Ernie Wise asked, "Why does he wear a bow tie? Because he trips all over the others."

Arthur Low declared, "Ordinary mortals after 50 years are presented with a gold watch. But we are privileged people who carry on till we drop."[2]

The following year, 1975, Arthur published his autobiography, *Before Your Very Eyes*, an 80,000-word surprisingly detailed and accurate record of his career. He was proud that the book, published on his 75th birthday, had not been ghost-written, responding to a fan, "I did write it myself. That's why it sounds as if I'm talking to the reader — as so many people have said."[3] In fact, Askey wrote the autobiography in long hand, and sister Rene typed it up for him in readiness for the publisher. (Similarly, Arthur would respond to fans in long hand, with Rene, in later years, typing them for him. As grand-daughter Jane recalls, "He was a great letter writer.")[4]

Wee Georgie Wood, of all people, reviewed the book in *The Stage* (June 19, 1975), and after complaining that he was only mentioned once and then only in passing, he continued,

"I've always looked up to Arthur — I've got to, he's bigger than me. Besides, he's been gifted with all the blessings the Almighty seems to bestow on Merseyside show folks from Robb Wilton Downwards.

"His book develops into a valid and fascinating portrait — warts and all — of a much, despite his lack of inches, larger than life personality, before one's very eyes, although those who know him intimately appreciate Askey is a much finer individual than his well chosen prose will disclose."

Arthur suffered a mild heart attack in September 1978, and was taken to the King Edward VII Hospital in Midhurst, Sussex. He assured his fans that he was "raring to get back" to work.

In July 1982, doctors at St. Thomas' Hospital, London, diagnosed that Arthur had a circulation problem identified

Arthur reads his autobiography to his grandson "Willy".

as gangrene in his left leg, and on Thursday, July 15, the leg was amputated. It was reported that he was "in very good form after the operation," and photographs were released showing the comedian in bed, surrounded by his nurses, and with a grin on his face. He told his agent that he could still work and was available to play Long John Silver. Askey's sense of humor was apparent as he responded to messages wishing him well on hospital stationary headed "The Maternity Ward." Sadly, a month later, the toes of Arthur's right leg were amputated, and on Sunday, October 2, 1982, he lost the right leg itself. Arthur Askey died on November 16, 1982, ready to face "the great adventure in the sky," as he called it.

He was "chirpy to the end," reported *The Guardian* (November 17, 1982), while the *Daily Mail* (April 20, 1980) quoted Askey as presciently commenting, "I've had a good life."

Askey's estate was announced to be worth 283,867 pounds gross and 266,828 net. Probate was granted to his son-in-law William Stewart (Anthea's husband) and to Lloyds Bank. The body was cremated at Putney Vale Cemetery and Crematorium, Wimbledon.

A Service of Thanksgiving for the Life and Work of Arthur Askey was held at the church of St. Martin-in-the-Field on Trafalgar Square on

With daughter Anthea after suffering a heart attack.

Thursday, March 24, 1983. There was a reading by actor Anthony Quayle and an address by Dickie Henderson. The final hymn was "Onward Christian Soldiers," and as the congregation dispersed, the organist played Lennon and McCartney's "Yesterday." The event was organized by the Saints and Sinners Club, a gentlemen's club for media, entertainment and political types, of which Askey was a pioneer member.

Daughter Anthea and sister Rene attend the Thanksgiving service for Arthur on March 24, 1983.

Anthea had initially wished to scatter her father's ashes at three theatres which had played a prominent part in his life, the London Palladium, the Alexandra Theatre, Birmingham, and the Richmond Theatre. Ultimately, she scattered the ashes at an unidentified beach, "where he had enormously happy times when I was a child and where I saw him laugh as much as I have ever seen him laugh."[5] Granddaughter Jane identifies the beach as being near her mother's house in West Sussex.[6] Anthea was successful in placing a plaque in Askey's honor at the Richmond Theatre, where the previous year he had played his last pantomime. Lesley Crowther and Roy Hudd were present on that occasion, but it would seem the plaque was taken down when the theatre had some restoration work done. Arthur was also honored with a blue plaque at the BBC Radio Theatre at Broadcasting House, unveiled on October 11, 1998.

Anthea insisted that her father had wanted her to write his biography — "he wanted me to tell the full story he couldn't write about himself" — but nothing came of the book, to be titled *The Sweetness and the Sorrow*.[7]

1. Arthur Askey, *Before Your Very Eyes*, p. 189.
2. Lynda Lee-Porter, "Simply the Nicest Man I Ever Knew."
3. Undated, handwritten postcard to unidentified fan, Anthony Slide Collection.
4. Jane Stewart to Anthony Slide, e-mail dated March 12, 2020.
5. Fred Norris, "My Dad…Oh How I Miss Him," p. 6.
6. Jane Stewart to Anthony Slide, e-mail dated February 20, 2020.
7. Fred Norris, "My Dad…Oh How I Miss Him," p. 6. In an e-mail, dated March 12, 2020, Jane Stewart comments, "She maybe had a few notes and ideas but nothing actually formally written. I know she talked about writing something a long time ago, but have never seen anything, other than bits and bobs of notes and memories in a variety of notebooks which we found after she passed away."

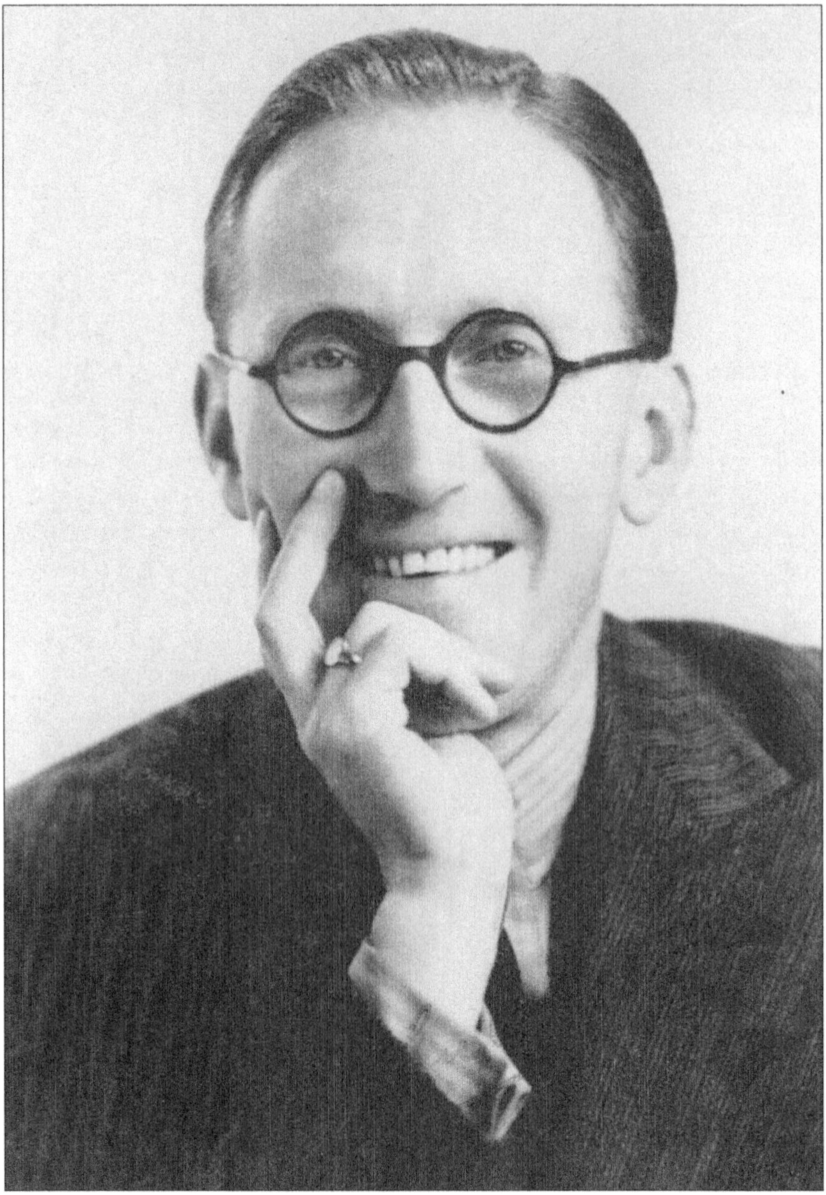

CHAPTER EIGHT

Legacy

In old age, there is no question that Askey became disenchanted with the new breed of comedians with whom he was competing for dates. "They're mostly all the same to me," he commented.

"Everyone is exactly the same. Just churning out jokes about Pakistanis, about infirmities…with their bracelets, and their elbows resting on the microphone stand. Nothing personable….They all look the same, too — dressed in evening suits, standing in front of a mike and telling the same jokes. In most of the clubs these days, all they learn is filth in a bad atmosphere. All people seem to want to go to clubs for these days is to booze! It's a pity."[1]

"Where do the young comedians come from? Now the club is the nursery, and it throws up computerized comics. They get the club feel that for me doesn't glitter at all. And then straight into the big money, money that I've never seen in my life. How long will it last…once they've done the set bit that they know?"[2]

He still had a positive word for one comedian — and that was fellow Liverpudlian Ken Dodd:

"Now there's a funny man! He'll get dressed up in a funny costume — just like the old music hall and variety days — and he's got the magic that the people love. There's not too much of that around now, unfortunately."[3]

Ken Dodd certainly had nothing but praise in public for Arthur Askey. He idolized Askey and would acknowledge *Band Waggon* as influential in his life and career. "Arthur Askey was like a firework display going off, so dynamic," said Dodd.[4] At the same time, Ken Dodd resented Askey's taking credit for the Diddy Men, and was dismissive of him (just as had been Ted Ray) as being nothing more than "a concert party turn."

Askey did not mince words when referring to modern stars, describing the Rolling Stones as "The Running Sores."[5] Described as "a fish out of water" when it came to pop stars, he would refer to Jerry and the Pacemakers as "Fred Pace and the Jerry Makers," a "jerry" being slang for a chamber pot.[6]

As Ken Dodd biographer, Louis Barfe, has written,

"A strange bitterness seems to pervade most of the interviews Askey gave in later life, giving the impression that he wasn't quite the big-hearted beacon of fun he made out on stage. And while Dodd was a lifelong Conservative, in interviews Askey sounded like he'd gone so far to the right that he'd fallen off some years earlier."[7]

Arthur shows his political colors in June 1975 as he poses with "The Bunny Girls" promoting Margaret Thatcher's platform that Free Enterprise Works.

There is a strong conservative streak to be found in the pages of Askey's autobiography, and at least one reviewer — in the July 2, 1975 edition of the *Belfast Telegraph* — wrote that "Askey's views are, in fact, forthright and conservative, almost to the point of being reactionary."

Arthur's grandchildren are united in their disagreement about his being an ultra-Conservative. Andrew writes,

"Certainly he was Conservative, but no more than Mum and Dad and they were certainly not 'extreme.' Yes he was pleased when Thatcher came to power and I think he admired her as a woman who 'got things done,' especially after the years of power cuts and rubbish in the streets. So, politically, I would say he was a Tory, but a very average, moderate Tory."[8]

As to Arthur's becoming crotchety in old age, granddaughter Jane responds at some length:

"I…happen to think that when many people reach their 60/70s or 80s and are still working, things have changed so much it becomes quite difficult as you start to feel like a fish out of water, even when you love what you're doing and is something you've devoted your whole life to….

"I never saw him irritable in old age, but instead tolerant and easy-going. He loved to spend any spare time he had with his family or on the golf course.

"I do however remember it mildly irritated him when people grabbed his hand like a vice and gave him a vigorous handshake, but this was because he was on Cortisone which thins the skin, and it caused him some discomfort and a great deal of bruising.

"Late on in his career he suffered with shingles which could maybe explain some irritability, as he continued working throughout until of course he was diagnosed with gangrene. I think he died from a broken heart having lost his wife many years earlier, and then after losing both legs and knowing his career was over.

"He actually continued to fight when he lost the first leg and had a prosthesis fitted and knowing him was probably filling a notebook with one legged jokes, but when he lost the second, he knew that his theatre years were over."[9]

A defiant and aging Arthur.

It must have been galling for Askey to find himself as a member of the supporting cast when American singer Vic Damone made his British debut at the London Palladium beginning on August 19, 1974, for a two week run. Around the same time, Askey was very much displeased when he met racist politician Enoch Powell at the opening of a Fleet Street pub and was asked, "What do you do?"

Certainly younger comedians resented Arthur Askey and any lasting appeal he might have. As one commentator noted in 1995,

"They work hard to create original, funny programmes, but are constantly reminded of the Golden Age of Radio Comedy and have to endure old farts banging on about The Goons and *ITMA* and Arthur Askey, even though many of these programmes are twee and unfunny to the contemporary comedy ear."[10]

Askey always insisted that making people laugh was his life, and it seemed to bother him little that the jokes hardly changed from one decade to the next. Harking back to the 1920s, in a way Arthur never ceased to be an end-of-the-pier comic. The jokes were never particularly topical. Unlike other comedians, he never had to read the morning papers to find material for his act. He was never slick or reduced himself to telling sick jokes that became popular as he approached old age. He never lost that energy that propelled him through life. As late as 1974, he was taking time out from a busy schedule in London to record a thirteen-part *Songs That Stopped the Show*, produced by Bill Younger for Tyne Tees Television in Newcastle.[11] Despite joking all day at the studio on- and off-camera until 10:30 p.m., he rejected the notion of relaxing at a hotel overnight, but would take the 11:05 sleeper train to London: "I don't want to waste the next day by staying overnight."

That same year, *The Times* hailed him as a "superb professional," describing Arthur as "a pioneer of the catchphrase and of much radio comedy, a pantomime dame of distinction, a star of films, command performances, reviews and television panel games."[12]

Askey always had goodwill with management, and that goodwill extended to his audience. He was always reliable, always on time, never throwing tantrums or threatening to walk out. For decades, his act on stage as a stand-up comic lasted for around forty minutes and seldom varied in length. Ken Dodd might go on stage and do five-and-a-half hours, leaving his audience exhausted. Arthur Askey did forty minutes and left his audience happy and perhaps wanting a little more (which was generally not forthcoming).

He never really slowed down. An extant diary from 1927 shows Askey's working 129 dates a year, everywhere from the Midland Grand to the Mecca, Ludgate Hill, and the Pembroke Hall, Croydon. A diary from 1964 shows his working 161 days of the year, including rehearsals and including, of course, Rhyl.

In 1975 Askey was asked about his approach to old age:

"I get my pension every week, but, working as much as I do, the Government claw it all back in tax. I can't grumble at 75 to be signed up for work for most of next year. I'm actually surprised when I hear myself say that I'm 75. The best thing you can have in old age is a bad memory. You don't keep reliving past times, chewing everything over."[13]

He was not that happy ultimately with his career, which he described as "a very steady livelihood," in regard to the money he made and might have made:

"I had hoped to leave my family quite a bit when I slide over, but there won't be all that much. Enough for them to have a good holiday in the South of France if they want it, but not much more….

"I was so blinded with success. I did a foolish thing. I made friends of my agent and my impresarios. We were all great mates. That's the wrong way. I don't say you've got to make enemies of your employers. But you don't want to be old friends.

"When I first hit it Jack Hylton brought the rights to *Band Waggon* from the BBC for the stage. He *couldn't* put it on without me. I could have screwed him to the ground but I didn't. The agent I had then was his pal and there was this little coterie down in Sussex. George Black from the Palladium was in it. And there was me, a little concert party lad. They *carved* me up. No doubt about it. I see it now. But what the hell…It's only when I hear of the fantastic sums the boys make now that I reflect a bit."[14]

How times and attitudes have changed albethey slowly. In 2000, a commentator in *The Stage* wrote,

"With his sheer good nature and ebullient good humour, Askey was widely regarded with immense affection, particularly during the darkest days of the Second World War. His infallible timing, infectious chuckle, sheer inventiveness and mischevious delight when a gag went wrong, forever endeared him to audiences and fellow cast members alike.

"Unlike many of those who followed, there was no malice in those twinkling eyes behind the thick-rimmed glasses."[15]

"Meeting Mr. Askey is a tonic," wrote a critic with the *Daily Express*, "and he's about the size of a Schweppes bottle. He still fizzes and sparkles inside his tumbler-thick glasses. And his laugh still sounds like the noise a paper donkey would make if it could feel the kids pinning on its tail."[16]

But the 21st Century is a very different time. The darkest days of the Second World War are long gone and cynical humor is more in need to deal with the current dark times the world is facing. "Forever" is an awfully long time, and the forever in which Arthur Askey has endeared himself to the British public has become yesterday. Tomorrow belongs to the vulgar and crude, to those comics recognizing that their audience has a chip on its collective shoulder, and basically to a world accepting that anything goes. It might well be argued that with the 2018 death of Ken Dodd, the "golden age" of British comedy died with him. The likes of John Cleese might believe themselves superior to the Ken Dodd and his ilk, but they have lost all touch with humor and with laughter, if they, particularly with John Cleese, ever were funny.

The most savage satire, although most will not understood who is being parodied, is the character of Arthur Atkinson, played by Paul Whitehouse on the BBC's *The Fast Show* (1994-1997). Arthur Atkinson is an incredibly unfunny and nonsensical stand-up comic with the catchphrases "How Queer" and "Where's Me Washboard?" (the one on which his heroin lost its flavor overnight). Shots of Arthur Atkinson are interspersed with old black-and-white footage of theatre audiences.

One modern comedian compared to Askey is Count Arthur Strong, played by creator Stephen Delaney. He is described as a "hopeless old-school variety performer, still trying to make it big in entertainment. Think Arthur Askey but without the charm or talent."[17]

The internet is rife with negative comments on Arthur Askey, some extremely crude and vulgar, and often referencing the amputation of his legs. He had become Arthur "Where's My Legs" Askey: "His act consisted of him rolling around the stage shouting 'I'm a fucking wasp.' Of course at this stage in his career he had lost his legs, hence the rolling."[18] "As a child, I always used to think that he wasn't very funny and assumed it was the sort of stuff that grown-ups found amusing. As I got older I realised that it was just that he wasn't very funny."[19] "Profoundly unfunny, something he shared with Will Hay, Ted Ray and the bloke with the jealous eyes that used to own Fulham FC [Football Club]."[20]

During his lifetime, in 1970, the National Portrait Gallery unveiled a gouache and pencil portrait or Arthur by Barry Fantoni. The artist, perhaps a strange choice to paint the conservative Askey, was a cartoonist and columnist for *Private Eye* and wrote scripts for the satirical *That Was the Week That Was*. In 1966, he had drawn caricatures for *Radio Times* and hosted a BBC show, *A Whole Scene Going On*, for which Fantoni was voted Television Personality of the Year.

In October 2018, "a wall of fame," honoring performers who had starred at the London Palladium was unveiled next to the theatre's stage door on Great Marlborough Street. A press release, rather sadly, noted, that "a tiny committee of people old enough to remember some of these artists" was put together to make the final choices, among whose number were Vera Lynn, Ken Dodd, Bruce Forsyth, and, of course, Arthur Askey.[21]

1. Geoff Leack, "Merseyside — Cradle of Show Business Talent," p. 177.
2. Horace Richards, "I Thang Yaw!"
3. Geoff Leack, "Merseyside — Cradle of Snow Business Talent," p. 177.
4. Louis Barfe, *Happiness and Tears,* p. 148.
5. *The Arthur Askey Variety Show,* programme three, recorded March 9, 1981.
6. John Vose, "Big-Hearted Arthur."
7. Ibid, p. 149.
8. Andrew Stewart to Anthony Slide, e-mail dated February 17, 2020.
9. Jane Stewart to Anthony Slide, e-mail dated February 17, 2020.
10. Arthur Smith, "Letter to a Young Comedian," p. 7.
11. *Songs That Stopped the Show* had a pub setting, with real drinks, and Arthur passing among the customers as a compere.
12. Kenneth Gosling, "Arthur Askey Still Superb Professional at 73."
13. "Six of the Oldest…and the Best," quotes from Wilfred Pickles, Renee Houston, Max Wall, Margaret Powell, Ella Milne, and Arthur Askey, unsourced clipping in Arthur Askey scrapbook.
14. Horace Richards, "I Thang Yow!"
15. John Martland, "Method in His Madness," p. 11.
16. Quoted in the *New York Times* obituary (November 17, 1982).
17. Claudia Connell, "Count Arthur Strong."
18. "Arthur Askey," *http://is-a-cunt.com.*
19. "The A-Z of Half Man Half Biscuit Arthur Askey."
20. Ibid. The Fulham Football Club owner is presumably Mohamed Al Fayed.
21. Robert Dex, "Palladium Honours Stars with Stage Door Wall of Fame," p. 8.

Bibliography

Articles cited without page numbers were found in the scrapbooks of Arthur Askey and had been inadequately sourced.

"The A-Z of Half Man Half Biscuit: Arthur Askey," *http://halfmanhalfbiscuit.co/uk/a-to-z-arthur-askey* (accessed April 2018).

"The Answers to Frowzy Sundays!," *Daily Herald*, March 27, 1954, p. 4.

"Arthur Askey," *http://is-a-cunt.com/2013/04/arthur askey/* (accessed August 2018).

Askey, Arthur, "Playmates — I Thank Yeaow!," *Liverpool Evening Express*, June 1, 1939, p. 4.

_____. *Before Your Very Eyes*. London: The Woburn Press, 1975.

"Arthur Askey," *The People*, January 8, 1939, p. 11.

"Arthur Askey: He Showed Symptoms of Being Able to Amuse," *Movietone News*, September 13, 2008, *http://www.movietone-news.com* (accessed April 2018).

"Arthur Askey Returns to Liverpool," *Liverpool Daily Post*, May 30, 1939, p. 4.

"Arthur Askey to Act in Comedy Here," *The Mail* (Adelaide), November 26, 1949, p. 2.

Arthur Askey's Album of Silly Little Songs. London: Chappell, undated.

"Askey's Impressions…of the Australian Theatre," *ABC Weekly*, November 25, 1950.

"The Band Waggon Show Guide," *http://www.britishcomedy.org.uk/ comedy/bandwaggon.htm* (accessed April 2018).

Barber, Lynne, "Beneath My Underpants I'm a Riot of Polka Dots and Moonbeams," *The Guardian*, August 19, 2000, *http://www.theguardian.com* (accessed December 2019).

Barfe, Louis. *Happiness and Tears: The Ken Dodd Story*. London: Apollo Books, 2019.

Barker, Dennis, "Anthea Askey: The Bite of the Showbiz Bug," *The Guardian*, March 28, 1999, *http://www.theguardian.com* (accessed April 2018).

Betts, Ernest, "Family Life of Arthur Askey, Radio Star of 1939," *Daily Mail*, date unknown.

Black, Peter, "Brilliant at 'Off the Cuff' Comedy, *TV Mirror*, March 26, 1955.

Blumenfeld, Simon, "There's Nothing Like a Dame," *The Stage*, December 19, 2002, p. 10.

Boswell, Josh and Parry, Ryan, "The Sad Last Picture of Sabrina, the British Answer to Marilyn Monroe," *Daily Mail*, October 13, 2017, *http://www.dailymail.co.uk* (accessed December 2019).

Brown, Geoff. *Walter Forde*. London: British Film Institute, 1977.

Brown, Mike. *Wartime Broadcasting*. Oxford, U.K.: Shire Publications, 2018.

Connell, Claudia, "Count Arthur Strong," *www.dailymail.co.uk* (accessed August 2018).

"Cryer the Beloved Stand-up Comedian," *The Stage*, December 15, 1954, p. 19.

Dex, Robert, "Palladium Honours Stars with Stage Door Wall of Fame," p. 8.

Faint, Pete. *Jack Hylton*. The Author, 2014.

Fisher, John. *Funny Way to Be a Hero*. London: Random House, 2013.

Fisher, John, and Tom Atkinson, director, *Comedy Heroes: Arthur Askey*. Thames Television, January 26, 1998.

Flanagan, Aubrey, "British Stars Who Beat the Bombers," *Motion Picture Herald*, January 3, 1942, p. 35.

Gifford, Denis. *The Golden Age of Radio*. London: B.T. Batsford, 1985.

_____. *Entertainers in British Films: A Century of Showbiz in the Cinema*. Westport, Ct.: Greenwood Press, 1998.

Goldie, Grace Wyndham, "Our Arthur," *The Listener*, December 1938, p. 1202.

Goodgans, L. Beswick, "Thanks for the Memory," *The Era*, December 30, 1938, p. 13.

Gosling, Kenneth, "Arthur Askey Still Superb Professional at 73," *The Times* (London), March 1, 1974.

Grand, Elaine, "Good Time Dames," *Nova*, December 1974, pp. 74-77.

Guest, Val. *So You Want to Be in Pictures*. London: Reynolds & Hearn, 2001.

Haley, Jim, "Revolution in Pantoland," *Plays and Players*, December 1977, pp. 12-15.

Harty, Russell. *Russell Harty Plus*. London: Abacus, 1974.

"How Askey Coined It In," *The Stage*, May 16, 2002, p. 12.

"Introducing Arthur Askey the Man Who Made *Band Waggon*," *Home and Empire*, April 1939.

Jarski, Rosemarie. *The Wit and Wisdom of the North*. London: Ebury Press, 2009.

Jeans, Angela. *The Man Who Was My Husband: A Biography of John Watt*. London: Vision Press, 1964.

Keegan, Natalie, "Star's Tragic End," *The Sun*, October 11, 2017, http://www.thesun.co.uk (accessed December 2019).

Leack, Geoff, "Merseyside — Cradle of Show Business, Talent," *The Stage*, January 31, 1980, p. 177.

Lee-Porter, Lynda, "Simply the Nicest Man I Ever Knew," *Daily Mail*, November 17, 1982.

Logan, Pamela W. *Jack Hylton Presents*. London: British Film Institute, 1995.

"The Little Man," *Coventry Evening Telegraph*, February 27, 1945, p. 2.

Lomas, Janice. *The Home Front in Britain: Images, Myths and Forgotten Experiences Since 1914*. Springer, 2014.

Marriott, R.B., "*Band Waggon* Begins," *The Era*, August 31, 1939, p. 7.

Martland, John, "Method in His Madness," *The Stage*, June 1, 20000, p. 11.

McCann, Graham, "Jimmy Clitheroe," *British Comedy Guide*, February 10, 2020, *www.comedy.co.uk* (accessed February 2020).

McKay, Mark, "Radio: Band Waggon," *https://laughterlog.com/2009/02/25/band-waggon/* (accessed September 2018).

"Meet BigHearted Arthur," *The People*, January 8, 1939, p. 11.

Melville, Alan. *Merely Melville*. London: Hodder and Stoughton, 1970.

Midwinter, Eric. *Make 'Em Laugh*. London: George Allen & Unwin, 1979.

Moreton, Angela, "New Little Man Joins Select Club," *The Stage*, December 28, 1967, p. 10.

Nicholas, Sadie, "Norma Ann Sykes: The Sad Decline of Britain's Marilyn Monroe," *Daily Express*, October 12, 2017, *http://www.express.co.uk* (accessed December 2019).

Nicholson, Patrick, "Little Big Man," *The Sunday Times* [London] *Magazine*, August 4, 1974, pp. 8-17.

Norris, Fred, "My Dad…Oh How I Miss Him," *Liverpool Echo*, January 18, 1983, p. 6.

"Okay to Kid Hitler on British Radio," *Variety*, October 4, 1939, p. 19.

"The Pantomime Tradition," *Illustrated London News*, November 2, 1975, pp. 12-13.

Richards, Horace, "Ay Thang Yow!," *Woman's Own*, February 3, 1974.

Rose, Clarkson, "Peradventure," *The Stage*, September 6, 1934, p. 2.

Saxon, Flaen, "Arthur Askey was an Utter and Total Cuntybollocks," *http://is-a-cunt.com* (accessed July 2018).

Scott, Will, "Now! Now! Now!," *Daily Herald*, March 18, 1939, p. 8.

Smith, Arthur, "Letter to a Young Comedian," *The Stage*, December 21, 1995, p. 7.

"Success of Odeon Sunday Concert," *Reading Mercury*, February 18, 1939, p. 5.

Tatchell, Peter, "Performers: Arthur Askey," Laughterlog.com (accessed May 2018).

_____, "Radio: Does the Team Think?," Laughterlog.com (accessed February 2019).

"Tuner," "*Band Waggon* Farewell," *Birmingham Daily Gazette*, March 15, 1939, p. 8.

Tynan, Kenneth, "It Made Me Weep," *Daily Sketch*, November 13, 1953.

Vose, John, "Big-Hearted Arthur," *http://www.bestofbritishmagazine.co.uk/big-hearted-arthur* (accessed April 2018).

Webb, Simon. *The Colchester Book of Days*. Stroud, United Kingdon: The History Press, 2013.

Welsh, Paul, "Elstree's Contribution to Erotic Cinema History," *Borehamwood & Elstree Times*, October 18, 2013, *http://www.borehamwoodtimes.co.uk* (accessed May 2018).

Whitfield, June. *....and June Whitfield*. London: Bantam Press, 2000.

"Who Invents the Jokes for *Band Waggon*?" *Radio Times*, November 3, 1939.

Young, Cy, "Sabrina: Model and Old-School Sex Symbol of 1950s British TV,"

The Independent, October 6, 2017, *http://independent.co.uk* (accessed December 2019).

Filmography

Calling All Stars. British Lion. *Released March 1937.* Director: Herbert Smith. With Davy Burnaby, B.C. Hilliam, Malcolm MacEarchen, and Ambrose and His Orchestra. As Waiter. 75 MINUTES. *Reissued 1943.*

Pathe Pictorial No. 43. British Pathe. As Himself. *Released 1937.* 10 MINUTES.

Pathe Pictorial No. 89. British Pathe. As Himself. *Released 1937.* 10 MINUTES.

Pathe Pictorial No. 115. British Pathe. As Himself. *Released 1938.* 10 MINUTES.

Band Waggon. Gainsborough. *Released January 1940.* Director: Marcel Varnel. Screenplay: Marriott Edgar, Val Guest, J.O.C. Orton, and Robert Edmunds. With Richard Murdoch, Jack Hylton, Pat Kirkwood, Moore Marriott, Peter Gawthorne, and Wally Patch. As Big Hearted Arthur. 85 MINUTES.

Charley's (Big-Hearted) Aunt. Gainsborough. *Released April 1940.* Director: Roy Boulting. Screenplay: Val Guest, Ralph Smart and J.O.C. Orton, based on the play by Brandon Thomas. With Richard Murdoch, Moore Marriott, Graham Moffatt, Phyllis Calvert, and Jeanne de Casalis. As Arthur Linden. 76 MINUTES.

Pathe Gazette No. 36. British Pathe. As Himself. *Released 1940.* 10 MINUTES.

The Ghost Train. Gainsborough. *Released February 1941.* Director: Walter Forde. Screenplay: Marriott Edgar, Val Guest and J.O.C. Orton, based on the play by Arnold Ridley. With Richard Murdoch, Kathleen Harrison, Morland Graham, Linden Travers, and Herbert Lomas (Herbert Lom). As Tommy Gander. 85 MINUTES. *Reissued 1947.*

I Thank You. Gainsborough. *Released August 1941.* Director: Marcel Varnel. Screenplay: Marrott Edgar and Val Guest. With Richard Murdoch, Moore Marriott, Graham Moffatt, Lily Morris, Kathleen Harrison, and Issy Bonn. As Arthur. 81 MINUTES.

Back Room Boy. Gainsborough. *Released April 1942.* Director: Herbert Mason. Screenplay: Val Guest, Marriott Edgar and J.O.C. Orton. With Moore Marriott, Graham Moffatt, Googie Withers, Vera Francis, and Joyce Howard. 82 MINUTES.

The Nose Has It. Gainsborough. As Arthur Pilbeam. *Released August 1942.* Director and Screenplay: Val Guest. 7 MINUTES.

King Arthur Was a Gentleman. Gainsborough. *Released December 1942.* Director: Marcel Varnel. With Evelyn Dall, Anne Shelton, Max Bacon, Jack Train, and Peter Graves. As Arthur King. 99 MINUTES.

Miss London Ltd. Gainsborough. *Released May 1943.* Director: Val Guest. Screenplay: Val Guest and Marriott Edgar. With Evelyn Dall, Anne Shelton, Richard Hearne, Max Bacon, and Jack Train. As Arthur Bowman. 99 MINUTES.

Bees in Paradise. Gainsborough. *Released March 1943.* Director: Val Guest. Screenplay: Val Guest and Marriott Edgar. With Anne Shelton, Peter Graves, Max Bacon, Jean Kent, and Ronald Shiner. As Arthur Tucker. 75 MINUTES.

New Pictorial. No. 48. British Pathe. *Released 1945.* As Himself. 10 MINUTES.

Arthur Askey on Going to the Dentist: No. 1, The Appointment. Public Relations Films for Lever Brothers. *Released 1947.* Director and Screenplay: Richard Massingham. With Russell Waters. As Himself. 2 MINUTES (200 ft.).

Arthur Askey on Going to the Dentist: No. 2, The Journey. Public Relations Films for Lever Brothers. *Released 1947.* Director and Screenplay: Richard Massingham. As Himself. 2 MINUTES (200 ft.).

Arthur Askey on Going to the Dentist: No. 3, The Waiting Room. Public Relations Films for Lever Brothers. *Released 1947.* Director and Screenplay: Richard Massingham. As Himself. 2 MINUTES (200 ft.).

[There are no onscreen credits for the above three short subjects produced as advertising films for Gibbs SR toothpaste. It is possible there is a fourth film in the series, titled Black and White, *but it does not appear to exist.]*

The Love Match. Group 3/Beaconsfield. *Released February 1955.* Director: David Paltenghi. Screenplay: Geoffrey Orme and Glenn Melvyn, based on the play by Glenn Melvyn. With Thora Hird, Glenn Melvyn, Robb Wilton, Shirley Eaton, and James Kenney. As Bill Brown. 85 MINUTES.

Ramsbottom Rides Again. Jack Hylton/British Lion. *Released May 1956.* Director: John Baxter. Screenplay: John Baxter, Basil Thomas, Arthur Askey, Glenn Melvyn, and Geoffrey Orme, based on the play by Harold G. Robert. With Glenn Melvyn, Sidney James, Shani Wallis, Frankie Vaughan, Betty Marsden, and Jerry Desmonde. As Bill Ramsbottom. 93 MINUTES.

The Lancashire Coast. British Transport Films. *Released August 1957.* Director: John Taylor. Screenplay: Cyril Ray. With Hubert Gregg and Stanley Holloway. As Himself. Documentary. 16 MINUTES.

Make Mine a Million. Elstree/British Lion. *Released February 1959.* Director: Lance Comfort. Screenplay: Peter Blackmore and Talbot Rothwell, based on a story by Jack Francis. With Sidney James, Dermot Walsh, Olga Lindo, Clive Morton, and Sally Barnes. As Arthur Ashton. 82 MINUTES.

Friends and Neighbours. Valiant/British Lion. *Released November 1959.* Director: Gordon Parry. With Megs Jenkins, Tilda Thamar, Peter Illing, Reginald Beckwith, and June Whitfield. As Arthur Grimshaw. 79 MINUTES.

The Alf Garnett Saga. Associated London Films/Columbia. *Released August 1972.* Director: Bob Kellett. Screenplay: Johnny Speight, based on the BBC Television series. With Warren Mitchell, Dandy Nichols, Adrienne Posta, John Le Mesurier, and Roy Kinnear. As Himself. 90 MINUTES.

To See Such Fun. Rank Organization. *Released December 1977.* Director: Jon Schoffield. With Frank Muir, George Formby, Will Fyffe, Tony Hancock, and Tommy Handley. As Himself. Documentary. 90 MINUTES.

Rosie Dixon — Night Nurse. Multiscope/Columbia. *Released February 1978.* Director: Justin Cartwright. Screenplay: Christopher Wood and Justin Cartwright, based on the novel by Rosie Dixon. With Debbie Ash, Caroline Argyle, Beryl Reid, John Le Mesurier, and Liz Fraser. As Mr. Arkwright. 88 MINUTES.

The Pantomime Dame. Arts Council of Great Britain. *Released December 1982.* Director: Elizabeth Wood. With Douglas Byng, Billy Dainty, George Lacey, Terry Scott, and Jack Tripp. As Himself. Documentary. 47 MINUTES.

Index

Agate, James, 97-98
Aladdin, 105
Aladdin and His Wonderful Lamp, 107
Alan Melville Takes You from A to Z, 128
The Alf Garnett Saga, 156
"All to Specification," 42, 68
Arthur Askey on Going to the Dentist, 154-155
The Arthur Askey Show, 58, 127
Arthur Askey's Annual, 19
Arthur's Anniversary, 125
Arthur's Inn, 61
Arthur's Treasured Volumes, 127
Ash, Debbie, 92
Askey, Anthea, 42, 43, 44. 58, 61, 90, 103, 109, 110, 111-114, 125, 127, 128, 134, 137, 139
Askey, Arthur, birth, 27; catchphrases, 20, 51; contracts, 39-40; death, 136-137; early years, 27-31; film career, 65-93; glasses, 11; marriage, 35; OBE and CBE, 134-135; pantomime career, 99-107; politics, 28, 142; radio career, 47-63; recordings, 55, 68-69; royal command performances, 107-108; size, 10-11; songs, 16, 34, 38-39, 42, 68-69, 95-96, 111; stage career, 95-116; television career, 119-130; theme song, 16
Askey, Irene (Rene), 27, 29, 134, 138
Askey Galore, 60
Askitoff, 18
Aspinall, Miss, 28
Atlantic Spotlight, 60
Australia, 109-110

Babes in the Wood, 39, 101, 103, 105, 107
Back-Room Boy, 75-76, 154
Bacon, Max, 76, 79, 80, 81

Band Waggon, 14, 19, 20, 38, 47-58. 60, 62, 96, 120, 145
Band Waggon (film), 66-68, 70, 72, 82, 153
Barnard, Cecil, 33
Baxter, John, 87, 89, 90
"The Bee Song," 38, 42, 62
Bees in Paradise, 80-83, 154
Before Your Very Eyes, 120-121, 123, 125
Before Your Very Eyes (autobiography), 135
Bet Your Life, 110
"Big-Hearted Arthur," 16, 65
Big Time, 60
Big's Broadcast, 60
Bird, Richard, 110, 111
Black, Edward, 68
Blackpool's Own Band Waggon, 56
Blain, Kenneth, 38-39
Block, Bob, 61
Bonn, Issy, 52, 74
The Boy Who Lost His Temper, 95-96
Bromley-Taylor, Rica, 95
Brown, Geoff, 16
"The Budgerigar," 69, 108
"Bumpity Bump," 15
Bygraves, Max, 135

Calling All Stars, 43, 65, 153
"Carry On" Films, 13, 90, 91
Cartwright, Justin. 92
Catchphrases, 20
Chaplin, Charlie, 15, 97
Charley's (Big-Hearted) Aunt, 70-72, 153
Cinderella, 103, 104, 107
Clitheroe, Jimmy, 9, 10
The Clitheroe Kid, 9
Colin, Sid, 59, 120

Comfort, Lance, 89
Concert Parties, 33-40
Coombs, Pat, 58, 60
Cooper, Tommy, 104, 119
Corbett, Ronnie, 9
The Coronation Review, 48
Crier, Gordon, 49, 53
Crump, Freddie, 78
Currys Radios, 18

Dahl, Evelyn, 76, 77, 78, 99
de Casalis, Jeanne, 70, 71
Dearden, Guy, 42
"The Death Watch Beetle," 60, 108
Desert Island Discs, 62
Desmonde, Jerry, 88-89
Dick Whittington, 101, 103, 107
Do You Mind?, 62
Dodd, Ken, 14, 25, 26, 27, 141-142, 144, 145
Does the Team Think?, 62
Drake, Charlie, 20, 130

Eaton, Shirley, 85-86, 121
Edgar, Marriott, 73, 75, 76, 78
Eight Bells, 43
Empire Broadcasts, 43
Everton Football Club, 29
"Every Little Piggy's Got a Curly Tail," 42, 69

Fantoni, Barry, 146
Fields, Gracie, 57-58
"The Filberts," 35-36
"The Flu Germ," 84
Fol-de-Rols, 96
Follow the Girls, 99
Forde, Walter, 73, 99
Formby, George, 53, 56, 71
Francis, Vera, 75
Franklyn, William, 86
Fred Clement;s Pantomime Productions Limited, 39-40, 101
Fred Wildon's Entertainers, 40, 41
Friends and Neighbours, 91, 155
Fyffe, Will, Jr., 114

Gay, Noel, 97
The Ghost Train, 11, 72-73, 75, 154
Gibbs SR Toothpaste, 84
Going to the Dentist, 84

Golders Green Hippodrome, 103, 104
Goodwin, Denis, 58, 60
Goody Two Shoes, 110
Gordon, Barbara, 108
Grade, Lew, 102-103
Grand National. 110
Graves, Peter, 77, 78, 79, 80
Greatrex Newman (London), 40
Grey, Monsewer Eddie, 101, 113, 114, 115
Guest, Val, 70, 73, 74, 76, 78, 80, 83, 107
H.M.V Recordings, 43, 55, 68-69
Hancock, Tony, 12
Handley, Tommy, 20, 25, 34. 47, 48, 58, 114
"Hands, Knees and Boomps-a-Daisy, 51, 68, 69
Harding, Bill, 61
Harris, Vernon, 49, 53
Harrison, Kathleen, 72, 74
Hay, Will, 11
Headgate Electric Theatre, 36
Hearne, Richard, 79, 80
Hello Playmates, 60
"Hello to the Sun," 74
Henderson, Dickie, 120-121, 127, 130, 138
Hercules Cycles, 18
Henman, Geoffrey, 95
Henry, Leonard, 47, 48
Hercules Cycles, 18
High Tide, 115
Holiday Camp, 119
How Do You Do?, 60-61
Howard, Joyce, 75
Humperdinck, Engelbert, 100, 105
Humpty Dumpty, 103
A Hundred Years of Humphrey Hastings, 128-129
Hylton, Jack, 55, 59-60, 62, 67, 68, 87, 89, 90, 99, 102, 110, 111, 124, 125, 127, 145

I Thank You, 73-74, 154
"I've Got Nothing To Do," 39

Jack and Jill, 101, 102
Jack and the Beanstalk, 105, 107
James, Sid, 87, 90, 105
John Sherman's Music Hall, 43
"Jovial Jesters," 33, 34

"Keep a Sunbeam in Your Pocket," 80
Kent, Jean, 80
The Kid from Stratford, 108-109

INDEX

King Arthur Was a Gentleman, 75, 76-78, 154
Kirkwood, Pat, 68
Koringa, 82

The Lancashire Coast, 155
Langley, Percival, 39
Lee, Vanessa, 51, 60, 77
Let's Go to Town, 54
Little Miss Muffet, 37
Little Tich, 9
Littlewoods, 18
Liverpool, 25-31
Liverpool Cathedral, 28-29
Liverpool Institute for Boys, 29
Liverpool Municipal Education Department, 26, 30
Living It Up, 58-59
Lom, Herbert, 72, 113
London Palladium, 55, 56, 103, 104, 105, 138, 143, 145
Love and Kisses, 124-125
The Love Match (film), 84-87, 91, 155
The Love Match (play), 111-112
The Love Racket, 97-99, 109
Low, Arthur, 135
Lupino, Stanley, 97
Lynn, Vera, 134, 146

Make Mine a Million, 89-90, 155
Marriott, Moore, 67, 70, 74, 75, 76, 83
Martini Vermouth, 17
Massingham, Richard, 84
McCartney, Paul, 30
Melville, Allan, 61, 128
Melvyn, Glenn, 84, 85, 86, 87, 89, 112, 125
Merson, Billy, 121, 123, 128
Ministry of Health, 83
Miss London Ltd, 38, 76, 78-80, 154
Moffatt, Graham, 70, 74, 75, 76, 83
Monkhouse, Bob, 16, 58, 60
Morris, Lily, 74
"The Mosquito," 38
"The Moth," 38, 65, 69
Mullard, Arthur, 127
Murdoch, Richard, 13, 17, 18, 20. 48-51, 55, 56, 58, 62, 68-70, 72, 73, 74, 83, 96

New Pictorial, 154
Newman & Beachcroft, 39

Ninety Years On, 128
Niven, David, 43, 60
Nixon, David, 62
The Nose Has It, 83, 154

Orme, Geoffrey, 84
Orton, J.O.C., 70, 75

Paltenchi, David, 86-87
Pantomime, 99-107
Pantomime Dame, 100
The Pantomime Dame, 156
Parnell, Val, 20
Parry, Gordon, 91
Pathe Gazette, 153
Pathe Pictorial, 38, 65, 153
Pinder, Powis, 40, 43
"The Pixie," 10, 108
"A Pretty Little Bird," 38, 62
Priwin, Hans Wolfgang, 52
Professor Dosser's Academy of Dance, 28
"The Proposal," 50, 55, 62

Radio Fun Annual, 19
Radio Luxembourg, 17-18
Raise Your Glasses, 128
Ramsbottom Rides Again, 87-89, 91, 123, 155
Ray, Ted, 14, 146
Reece, Brian, 61, 110
Rhyl, 33-34, 144
Richard, Cliff, 105
Richmond Theatre, 106, 138
Ridley, Arnold, 72
Robey, George, 47
Robin Hood, 104
Robinson Crusoe, 103-104, 105
Rogers, Gilbert, 33, 34
Ronson Lighters, 18
Rose, Clarkson, 37
Rosie Dixon -- Night Nurse, 13, 91-92, 156
Ross, Danny, 59, 84, 86, 87, 91, 111, 125
Rothwell, Talbot, 59, 90, 91, 120
Royal Command Performances, 107-108, 133
Rutherford, Robert, 42, 84

Sabrina, 60, 89, 90, 121-123, 125
St. Michael's-in-the-Hamlet Primary School 28
"The Scarlets," 35
Schmidt, Josef, 15

"The Seagull," 38
"The Seaside Band," 37-38, 69
Secombe, Harry, 134
Second Honeymoon, 128
Shanklin, 40, 43
Shaw, George Bernard, 97
She Shall Have Music, 59-60
Shelton, Anne, 76, 78, 80. 107
Shelton, Josie, 80
Shiner, Ronald, 77, 80, 81, 82
Shiver Me Timbers or the Irate Pirate, 43
Sinbad, 101
The Sleeping Beauty, 106
Smart, Ralph, 70
"Song Salad," 36-37, 39
Songs That Stopped the Show, 144
Southsea, 37, 114
Spencer, Dennis, 114
Stewart, William, 112
Studio Hotel, 83
Swash, Elizabeth May, 18, 35, 39, 133-134
Sykes, Eric, 135
Symington's Soups, 17

Talk of the Town, 124
Television Christmas Party, 119
"Thanks for Dropping in Mr. Hess," 69
Thatcher, Margaret, 142
This Is Your Life, 29, 130
Thomas, Basil, 108
Thomas, Brandon, 70, 72
To See Such Fun, 156
Torquay, 82, 96
Train, Jack, 77, 78

Trinder, Tommy, 48, 52, 55, 56, 62
TV Fun, 19
Tynan, Kenneth, 111-112

Vaughan, Frankie, 89
Varnel, Marcel, 66, 73
Vetchinsky, Alex, 67
Victoria Palace, 97, 99, 111

Walker, Syd, 51, 55, 58
Wallis, Shani, 87, 89
Wall, Max, 56
Ward, Bill, 121
Watt, John 48-49, 50, 56
"We're Going to Hang Out the Washing on the Siegfried Line," 68-69
Welsh Infantry Regiment, 31
West, Gracie, 9
West Ham United Football Club, 29
What a Racket!, 114-115
Whitehouse, Paul, 146
Whitfield, David, 100, 103-104
Whitfield, June, 16-17, 91, 119, 125, 126, 127, 130
Wilcox, Frank, 42
Wilton, Robb, 25, 86, 124
Wise, Ernie, 11, 56
Withers, Googie, 75, 76
Wood, Wee Georgie, 9, 10, 136
"The Worm," 38-39, 68
Worth, Penny, 49, 53

Yule, Fred, 58

About the Author

British-born ANTHONY SLIDE is the author or editor of more than 200 books on the history of popular entertainment. He published his first book, *Early American Cinema*, in 1970, and since then he has written pioneering volumes on many subjects. Two of his books, *The American Film Industry: A Historical Dictionary* (1986) and *The Encyclopedia of Vaudeville* (1994) have been named Outstanding Reference Source of the Year by the American Library Association. His *"It's the Pictures That Got Small: Charles Brackett on Billy Wilder and Hollywood's Golden Age* (2014) was named one of the Outstanding Books of the Year by *The Guardian* newspaper.

He is particularly noted for his work on female film directors of the silent era, having written books on *Early Women Directors* (1997, and later revised as *The Silent Feminists*) and *Lois Weber: The Director Who Lost Her Way in History* (1996), edited *The Memoirs of Alice Guy Blaché* (1996), and co-produced, written and directed *The Silent Feminists: America's First Women Directors* (1993).

He is on-screen commentator and Consulting Producer of the 2018 feature film *Be Natural: The Untold Story of Alice Guy Blanché.*

Anthony Slide is the former resident film historian of the Academy of Motion Picture Arts and Sciences and associate film archivist of the American Film Institute. In 1990, he was awarded a honorary doctorate of letters by Bowling Green State University, and at that time he was hailed by Lillian Gish as "our pre-eminent historian of the silent era."

Among his other books for BearManor Media are *Frank Lloyd: Master of Screen Melodrama* (2009), *A Man Named Smith: The Novels and Screen Legacy of Thorne Smith* (2010) and *Wake Up at the Back There!: It's Jimmy Edwards* (2018).

Printed in Great Britain
by Amazon